I would like ...	**Vorrei ...** vōre'ē ...
How much does this cost?	**Quanto costa?** kōō-än'tō kō'stä?
Could you please write that down for me?	**Me lo può scrivere, per favore?** me lō pōō-ō' skrē'vere, per fävō're?
Where is ...?	**Dov'è ...?** dōve' ...?
Where is/are there ...?	*Dov'èl**Dove sono ...?** dōve'/dō've sō'nō ...?*
Today.	**Oggi.** ō'jē.
Tomorrow.	**Domani.** dōmä'nē.
I don't want to.	**Non voglio.** nōn vō'lyō.
I can't.	**Non posso.** nōn pō'sō.
Just a minute, please.	**Un momento, per favore!** ōōn mōmen'tō, per fävō're!
Leave me alone!	**Mi lasci in pace!** mē lä'shē ēn pä'tshe!

Name
Nome
Home address
Indirizzo di residenza

Date of birth
Data di nascita
Vacation address
Indirizzo di vacanza

ID/passport no.
Numero *della carta d'identità/del passaporto*

In case of emergency, please contact:
In caso di emergenza avvisare:

Important information (allergies, medicines, blood type, etc.)
**Informazioni importanti (allergie, farmaci,
gruppo sanguigno ecc.)**

In case of lost traveler's checks, please contact:

In case of lost credit cards, please contact:

Langenscheidt's
Universal
Phrasebook
Italian

Edited by the
Langenscheidt Editorial Staff

LANGENSCHEIDT
NEW YORK · BERLIN · MUNICH
VIENNA · ZURICH

Phonetic transcriptions: The Glanze Intersound System
Illustrations: Helen Schiffer

Neither the presence nor the absence of a designation that any entered word constitutes a trademark should be regarded as affecting the legal status of any trademark.

© 1999 Langenscheidt KG, Berlin and Munich
Printed in Germany by Druckhaus Langenscheidt,
Berlin-Schöneberg

INHALT

3

4   FOOD AND DRINK

5   SIGHTSEEING

6   SHOPPING

7 ENTERTAINMENT AND SPORTS

10   TIME AND WEATHER

241   GRAMMAR

Numbers

HOW TO FIND IT

This phrasebook contains all of the most important expressions and words you'll need for your trip. They have been divided up according to situation and organised into 10 chapters. The page borders have been colored to help you find things even more quickly.

Each chapter consists of example sentences and lists of words together with complementary vocabulary. This will help you put together exactly the right sentence you need for any situation. The easy-to-understand basic grammar section will give you further support.

Of course you can just show the person you're talking to the Italian translation of the sentence you wish to say. But the easily distinguished, blue phonetic alphabet will enable you to speak your chosen phrase without any knowledge of Italian whatsoever.

For vital situations we have also included sentences that go from Italian to English, so that an Italian may also be able to communicate with you.

In order to cover as many different situations as possible, we offer alternatives with many sentences; these are written in italics and separated by a slash:

Will I see you *tomorrow/this evening*?   **Ci vediamo *domani/stasera*?**
tshē vedyä'mō *dōmän'ē/stäse'rä*?

9

You can separate the alternatives into individual sentences, asking either:

Will I see you tomorrow?	**Ci vediamo domani?** tshē vedyä'mō dōmän'ē?

or

Will I see you this evening?	**Ci vediamo stasera?** tshē vedyä'mō stäse'rä?

When we offer more than two possibilities there will be an ellipsis at that point in the sentence; the possible phrases to complete your sentence will be listed underneath:

I would like...	**Vorrei...** vōre'ē...
a list of hotels.	**un annuario alberghi.** ōōn änōō-är'yō älber'gē.
a map of the area.	**una cartina della zona.** ōō'nä kärtē'nä de'lä dzō'nä.
a map of the city.	**una pianta della città.** ōō'nä pyän'tä de'lä tshtä'.
a map of the subway.	**una cartina della metropolitana.** ōō'nä kärtē'nä de'lä metrōpōlētä'nä.
a calendar of events.	**un programma delle manifestazioni.** ōōn prōgrä'mä de'le mänēfestätsyō'nē.

You can then put them together as needed, for example:

I would like a map of the city.	**Vorrei una pianta della città.** vōre'ē ōō'nä pyän'tä de'lä tshtä'.

Often you will also find sentence completions in parentheses. You can include these in your communication as you like.

How much does this **Quanto costa (all'incirca)?**
cost (approximately)? kōō·än'tö kō'stä (älēntshĕr'kä)?

If you wish to know the exact price, then simply leave out the word for approximately - **all'incirca**.

In Italian the form of the word used is sometimes dependent upon the gender of either the person speaking or the person addressed. In these cases we have indicated the different forms by the symbols ♂ (masculine) and ♀ (feminine):

Are you married? **È ♂ sposato/ ♀ sposata?**
e ♂ spōzä'tö/ ♀ spōzä'tä?
You would ask a man: **È sposato?**, and a woman **È sposata?**

In Italian, nouns and their qualifying adjectives belong to either the masculine or feminine gender, and the articles differ accordingly. To clarify this we have used the abbreviations *m* for masculine and *f* for feminine words in the vocabulary lists. We have included the feminine endings with the adjectives only when they are irregular. You will find the rules for the regular endings in the short grammar section of this book.

We hope you enjoy using our phrasebook and have a fun-filled vacation!

11

HOW DO YOU PRONOUNCE IT?

All words and phrases are accompanied by simplified pronunciation. The sound symbols are the ones you are familiar with from your high-school or college dictionaries of the *English* language, but applied here to foreign languages – a unique feature of *Langenscheidt's Universal Phrasebooks*.

Symbol	Approximate Sound	Examples
	VOWELS	
ä	The *a* of *father*.	*facile* fä'tshēle
e	Either the *e* of *met* (as in Italian *festa*) or the *a* of *fate* (as in Italian *sera*). The difference is not shown here; it has to be learned by listening.	*festa* fe'stä *sera* se'rä
ē	The *e* of *he*.	*piccolo* pē'kōlō
ī	The *i* of *time*.	*dai* dī *traino* trī'no
ō	Either the *o* of *nose* (as in Italian *sole*) or the *o* of *often* (as in Italian *donna*). The difference is not shown here; it has to be learned by listening.	*sole* sō'le *donna* dō'nä

Symbol	Approximate Sound	Examples
oi	The *oi* of *voice*.	*poi* poi
ōō	The *u* of *rule* (but without the "upglide").	*luna* lōō'nä
ou	The *ou* of *house*.	*laudare* loudä're
	CONSONANTS	
b	The *b* of *boy*.	*bello* be'lō
d	The *d* of *do*.	*dare* dä're
f	The *f* of *far*.	*farina* färē'nä
g	The *g* of *go*.	*gusto* gōō'stō
j	The *j* of *John*.	*giorno* jōr'nō *oggetto* ōje'tō
k	The *k* of *key*, the *c* of *can*.	*casa* kä'sä *scherzo* sker'tsō
l	The *l* of *love* (not of *fall*).	*mela* me'lä
m	The *m* of *me*.	*mano* mä'nō
n	The *n* of *no*.	*nome* nō'me
ng	The *ng* of *sing*. (Occurs in some foreign words in Italian.)	*bowling* bō'lēng
p	The *p* of *pin*.	*pane* pä'ne

13

Symbol	Approximate Sound	Examples
r	The *r* of *run* (but with a slight "trill").	*roba* rō′bä *carta* kär′tä
s	The *s* of *sun* (See also *z*, below.)	*sala* sä′lä *casa* kä′sä
sh	The *sh* of *shine*.	*lasciare* läshä′re
t	The *t* of *toy*.	*tempo* tem′pō
tsh	The *ch* of *much*.	*cento* tshen′tō
v	The *v* of *vat*.	*vita* vē′tä
y	The *y* of *year*.	*gennaio* jenä′yō *stiamo* styä′mō
z	The *z* of *zeal*.	*paese* pä·e′ze *sbaglio* zbä′lyō

Note these frequent combinations:

ly	as in *meglio* me′lyō
ny	as in *agnello* änye′lō or *legno* le′nyō
ts	as in *rizzare* rētsä′re or *zampa* tsäm′pä
dz	as in *mezzo* me′dzō or *zebra* dze′brä
tsy	as in *negozio* negō′tsyō
ōō·e	as in *guerra* gōō·e′rä
ōō·ē	as in *qui* kōō·ē′ or *guidare* gōō·ēdä′re

A raised dot separates two neighboring vowel symbols. This dot is merely a convenience to the eye; it does not indicate a break in pronunciation.

14

Human Relations

HI AND BYE!

Good morning.	**Buongiorno!** bōō-ônjôr'nō!
Good afternoon.	**Buongiorno!** bōō-ônjôr'nō!
Good evening.	**Buona sera!** bōō-ô'nä se'rä!
Good night.	**Buona notte!** bōō-ô'nä nō'te!
Hi.	**Ciao!** tshäö!

INFO To greet someone during the late afternoon and evening, say **Buona sera**. **Buona notte** is used only very late in the evening before you go to bed. Say **Ciao** to greet good friends or acquaintances.

May I sit here?	**Posso sedermi accanto a *Lei/te*?** pō'sō seder'mē äkän'tô ä *le'ē/te*?
I'm sorry, but this seat is taken.	**No, mi dispiace, qui è già occupato.** nō, mē dēspyä'tshe, kōō-ē' e jä ōkōōpä'tō.
How are you?	**Come *sta/stai*?** kō'me *stä/stī*?
I'm sorry, but I have to go now.	**Mi dispiace, ma adesso devo andare.** mē dēspyä'tshe, mä äde'sō de'vō ändä're.
Good-bye!	**Arrivederci!** ärēveder'tshē!
So long/see you tomorrow!	**A *presto/domani*!** ä pre'stō/dōmä'nē!
Bye!	**Ciao!** tshäö!

16

To take your leave of good friends you say **Ciao**. The more "official" way to say goodbye is **Arrivederci**, or **Arrivederla** äreveder'lä if you wish to show particular respect to an individual person.

Nice meeting you.	**Molto piacere di *averLa conosciuta/* *averti conosciuto*.** môl'tō pyätshe're dē äver'lä kōnōshōō'tä/äver'tē kōnōshōō'tō.
Thank you for a lovely evening.	**Grazie per la bella serata.** grä'tsē·e per lä be'lä serä'tä.
Have a good trip!	**Buon viaggio!** bōō·ôn' vyä'jō!

SMALL TALK ...

... about yourself and others

What's your name?	**Come *si chiama/ti chiami*?** Kō'me sē kyä'mä/tē kyä'mē?
My name is ...	**Mi chiamo ...** mē kyä'mō ...

INFO There are three ways to say "you" in Italian: a familiar, a polite, and a plural form. The **tu** tōō (familiar) form is used when friends, children, and young people talk individually to each other. Use the **Lei** le'ē (polite) form when speaking to strangers, lesser-known acquaintances, or elders. And when addressing two or more people – regardless of how well you know them – use the **voi** vo'ē (plural) form.

Where are you from?	**Di *dov'è*/*dove sei*?** dē dōve'/dō've se'ē?
I'm from the United States.	**Sono ♂ americano/♀ americana.** sō'nō ♂ämerēkä'nō/♀ämerēkä'nä.
I'm from New York.	**Sono di New York.** sō'nō dē nōōyôrk'.
Are you married?	***È*/*Sei* ♂ sposato/♀ sposata?** e/se'ē ♂ spōzä'tō/♀ spōzä'tä?
Do you have children?	***Ha*/*Hai* figli?** ä/ī fē'lyē?
Do you have any brothers or sisters?	***Ha*/*Hai* dei fratelli?** ä/ī de'ē fräte'lē?
I have a *sister*/*brother*.	**Ho una sorella/un fratello.** ō ōō'nä sōre'lä/ōōn fräte'lō.
How old are you?	**Quanti anni *ha*/*hai*?** kōō·än'tē ä'nē ä/ī?
I'm ... old.	**Ho ... anni.** ō ... ä'nē.
What sort of work do you do?	**Che lavoro *fa*/*fai*?** ke lävō'rō fä/fī?
I'm still going to school.	**Vado ancora a scuola.** vä'dō änkō'rä ä skōō·ō'lä.

18

? **È la prima volta che *è/sei* qui?**
e lä prēmä vōl'tä ke *e/se'ē* kōō·ē'?

Is this your first time here?

No, I've been to Italy ... time(s) before.

No, sono ♂ stato/♀ stata in Italia già altre ... volte. nō, sō'nō ♂ stä'tō/♀ stä'tä ēn ētä'lyä jä äl'tre ... vōl'te.

? **Da quanto tempo *è/sei* qui?**
dä kōō·än'tō tem'pō *e/se'ē* kōō·ē'?

How long have you been here?

For ... days/ weeks now.

Da ... *giorni/settimane.*
dä ... jōr'ne/setēmä'ne.

? **Per quanto tempo *rimane/rimani* ancora?** per kōō·än'tō tem'pō rēmä'ne/rēmä'nē änkō'rä?

How much longer will you be staying?

I'm leaving tomorrow.

Riparto domani. rēpär'tō dōmä'nē.

Another week/ two weeks.

Ancora *una settimana/due settimane.*
änkō'rä ōō'nä setēmä'nä/dōō'e setēmä'ne.

? **Le/Ti piace qui?**
le/tē pyä'tshe kōō·ē'?

How do you like it here?

I like it very much.

Mi piace molto. mē pyä'tshe mōl'tō.

Have you seen ... ?

Ha/Hai già visto ...? ä/ī jä vē'stō ...

Have you ever been to America?	**È/Sei ♂ stato/♀ stata mai in America?** e/se'ē ♂ stä'tō/♀ stä'tä mī ēn äme'rēkä?
Did you like it there?	**Le/Ti è piaciuta?** le/tē e pyätshōō'tä?
You should visit me if you come to America.	**Mi venga/vieni a trovare, se viene/vieni in America.** mē ven'gä/vye'nē ä trōvä're, se vye'ne/vye'nē ēn äme'rēkä.
This is my address.	**Ecco il mio indirizzo.** e'kō ēl mē'ō ēndērē'tsō.
You're welcome to stay at my house.	**Può/Puoi venire a stare da me.** pōō·o'/pōō·oi've'nē're ä stä're dä me.
I'd love to show you the *city/town*.	**Le/Ti faccio vedere la città.** le/tē fä'tshō vede're lä tshētä'.

SOCIALIZING

Would you like to …?

What are you doing tomorrow?	**Che cosa fa/fai domani?** ke kō'sä fä/fī dōmä'nē?
We could do something together, if you like.	**Potremmo fare qualcosa insieme, se Le/ti va.** pōtre'mō fä're kōō·älkō'sä ēnsye'me, se le/tē vä.
Shall we meet *this evening/tomorrow*?	**Ci vediamo stasera/domani?** tshē vedyä'mō stäse'rä/dōmän'ē?

20

Yes, I'd like that.	**Sì, volentieri.** sē, vōlentyĕ′rē.

I'm sorry, but I already have plans.	**Purtroppo non posso, ho già un impegno.** pōōrtrō′pō nōn pō′sō, ō jä ōōn ēmpe′nyō.

INFO When addressing a man, use **signor** sēnyōr and his last name, if known. Women are addressed as **signora** sēnyō′rä, girls and younger women as **signorina** sēnyōrē′nä, with or without the last name.

Would you like to join me for dinner this evening?	**Andiamo a mangiare insieme stasera?** ändyä′mō ä mänjä′re ēnsye′me stäse′rä?

➡ *see also: Dining with Friends (p. 115), Going out in the Evening (p. 193)*

I'd like to invite you to …	**La/Ti vorrei invitare.** lä/tē vōrre′ē ēnvētä′re.

When/Where shall we meet?	***Quando/Dove* ci incontriamo?** kōō·än′dō/dō′ve tshe ēnkōntrē·ä′mō?

Let's meet at … o'clock.	**Incontriamoci alle …** ēnkōntrē·ämōtshe ä′le …

I'll pick you up at … o'clock.	**La/Ti vengo a prendere alle …** lä/tē ven′gō ä pren′dere ä′le …

I'll take you home.	**La/Ti accompagno a casa.** lä/tē äkōmpä′nyō ä kä′sä.

| Will I see you again? | **Ci vediamo un'altra volta?** |
| | tshē vedyä'mō ōōnäl'trä vōl'tä? |

No, thanks!

| I'm afraid that won't be possible. | **Mi dispiace, ma non posso.** |
| | mē dēspyä'tshe, mä nōn pō'sō. |

| I already have plans. | **Ho già un impegno.** |
| | ō jä ōōn ēmpe'nyō. |

| I'm waiting for someone. | **Aspetto qualcuno.** äspe'tō kōō·älkōō'nō. |

| I'm not interested. | **Non ho voglia.** nōn ō vō'lyä. |

| That's enough of that! | **Adesso basta!** äde'sō bä'stä! |

| Get lost! | **Sparisci!** spärē'shē! |

COMMUNICATING

| Does anyone here speak English? | **C'è qualcuno che parla inglese?** tshe kōō·älkōō'nō ke pär'lä ēn·gle'se? |

| ? *Parla/Parli* italiano? | Do you speak |
| *pär'lä/pär'lē* ētälyä'nō? | Italian? |

| Only a little. | **Soltanto un po'.** sōltän'tō ōōn pō. |

| Please speak a little more slowly. | **Per favore, parli più lentamente.** |
| | per fävō're, pär'lē pyōō lentämen'te. |

? *Ha/Hai* capito? ä/ī käpē'tō?   Do you understand?

I understand.	**Ho capito.** ō käpē'tō.
I didn't understand that.	**Non ho capito questo.** nōn ō käpē'tō kōō·e'stō.
Could you repeat that, please?	**Lo può ripetere, per favore?** lō pōō·ō' rēpe'tere, per fävō're?
What is this called in Italian?	**Come si dice in italiano?** kō'me sē dē'tshe ēn ētälyä'nō?
What does ... mean?	**Che cosa significa ...?** ke kō'sä sēnyē'fēkä ...?
Please write it down for me.	**Me lo scriva, per favore.** me lō skrē'vä, per fävō're?
How do you pronounce that?	**Come si pronuncia?** kō'me sē pronōōn'tshä?

What do you think?

It *was/is* very nice here.	**È stato/È molto bello qui.** e stä'tō/e mōl'tō be'lō kōō·ē'.
Great!	**Benissimo!** bene'sēmō!
Wonderful!	**Magnifico!** mänyē'fēkō!
I like that.	**Mi piace.** mē pyä'tshe.
Gladly.	**Molto volentieri.** mōl'tō vōlentye'rē.
OK.	**Va bene.** vä be'ne.

23

It's all the same to me.	**Mi è indifferente.** mē e ēndēferen'te.
Whatever you like.	**Come _vuole/vuoi._** kō'me vōō·ō'le/vōō·ōĬ
I don't know yet.	**Non lo so ancora.** nōn lō sō änkō'rä.
Maybe.	**Forse.** fōr'se.
Too bad!	**Che peccato!** ke pekä'tō!
I'm afraid that's impossible.	**Purtroppo non è possibile.** pōōrtrō'pō nōn e pōse'bēle.
I'd rather ...	**Preferirei ...** preferēre'ē ...
I don't like that.	**Non mi piace.** nōn mē pyä'tshe.
No.	**No.** nō.
Absolutely not.	**In nessun caso.** ēn nesōōn' kä'zō.

BASIC PHRASES

Please; Thank you

Could you please help me?	**Mi potrebbe aiutare, per favore?** mē pōtre'be äyōōtä're, per fävō're?
Yes, please.	**Sì, volentieri.** sē, vōlentye'rē.
No, thank you.	**No, grazie.** nō, grä'tsē·e.
Thank you very much.	**Grazie mille.** grä'tsē·e mē'le.

Thank you, that was very nice of you.	**Molte grazie, è stato molto gentile da parte Sua.** mōl'te grä'tsē·e, e stä'tō mōl'tō jentē'le dä pär'te sōō'ä.

You're welcome.	**Prego.** pre'gō.

INFO To say "please," use **per favore**. The Italian word **prego** means "you're welcome" when used as a response to **grazie** (thank you). It is, however, also used when giving or handing something to someone (like saying "Here you are") or indicating to someone to take a seat or go ahead ("After you").

May I?	**Posso?** pō'sō?

I'm sorry!

Excuse me!	**Scusi!** skōō'zē!
Sorry about that.	**Mi dispiace.** mē dēspyä'tshe.
It was a misunderstanding.	**È stato un malinteso.** e stä'tō ōōn mälēnte'zō.

Best wishes!

Best wishes!	**Tante belle cose!** tän'te be'le kō'sē!
Happy birthday!	**Tanti auguri di buon compleanno!** tän'tē ougōō'rē dē bōō·ōn' kōmple·ä'nō!
Have a good trip!	**Buon viaggio!** bōō·ōn' vyä'jō!

Have a good time!	**Buon divertimento!** bōō·ōn' dēvertēmen'tō!
Merry Christmas!	**Buon Natale!** bōō·ōn' nätä'le!
Happy New Year!	**Felice anno nuovo!** felē'tshe ä'nō nōō·ō'vō!
Happy holidays!	**Buone feste!** bōō·ō'ne fe'ste!

FOR THE HANDICAPPED

I'm physically handicapped. Can you please help me?	**Sono ♂ handicappato/♀ handicappata. Mi può aiutare, per favore?** sō'nō ♂ ändēkäpä'tō/♀ ändēkäpä'tä. mē pōō·ō' äyōōtä're, per fävō're?
Do you have a wheelchair for me?	**Ha una sedia a rotelle per me?** ä ōō'nä se'dyä ä rōte'le per me?
Can you please take my luggage to the *room/taxi*?	**Mi può portare i bagagli *in camera/fino al taxi*?** mē pōō·ō' pōrtä're ē bägä'lye *ēn kä'merä/fē'nō äl tä'ksē*?
Where is the nearest elevator?	**Dov'è l'ascensore più vicino?** dōve' läshensō're pyōō vētshē'nō?
Is it suitable for wheelchairs?	**È accessibile alle sedie a rotelle?** e ätshesē'bēle ä'le se'dye ä rōte'le?
Is there a ramp for wheelchairs?	**C'è una salita per sedie a rotelle?** tshe ōō'nä sälē'tä per se'dye ä rōte'le?

Where is the rest room for handicapped?	**Dov'è un gabinetto per handicappati?** dôve' ōōn gäbēne'tō per ändēkäpä'tē	
I need someone to accompany me.	**Ho bisogno di qualcuno che mi accompagni.** ō bēzō'nyō dē kōō-älkōō-nō ke mē äkōmpä'nyē	

Human Relations

address	**l'indirizzo** lēndērē'tsō
alone	**solo** sō'lō
to arrive	**arrivare** ärēvä're
boyfriend	**il ragazzo** ēl rägä'tsō
brother	**il fratello** ēl fräte'lō
brothers and sisters	**i fratelli** ē fräte'lē
child	**il bambino** ēl bämbē'nō
city	**la città** lä tshētä'
to go dancing	**andare a ballare** ändä're ä bälä're
daughter	**la figlia** lä fē'lyä
father	**il padre** ēl pä'dre
friend *(male)*	**l'amico** lämē'kō
friend *(female)*	**l'amica** lämē'kä
girlfriend	**la ragazza** lä rägä'tsä
to have plans	**avere un impegno** äve're ōōn ēmpe'nyō
husband	**il marito** ēl märē'tō
to invite	**invitare** ēnvētä're
to like *(I would like to)*	**volere** vōle're
to like *(it appeals to me)*	**piacere** pyä'tshere

27

to leave	**partire** pär'tē're
little	**poco** pô'ko
to make a date	**darsi appuntamento**
	där'sē äpoontämen'to
married	*sposato/sposata* spozä'to/spozä'tä
to meet	**conoscere** kono'shere
(get to know)	
to meet *(up with*	**incontrarsi** enkonträr'sē
someone)	
mother	**la madre** lä mä'dre
no	**no** no
to go out to eat	**andare a mangiare (fuori)**
	ändä're ä mänjä're (foo-o'rē)
profession	**la professione** lä profesyo'ne
satisfied	**contento** konten'to
school	**la scuola** lä skoo-o'lä
sister	**la sorella** lä sore'lä
son	**il figlio** ēl fē'lyo
to speak	**parlare** pärlä're
student *(female)*	**la studentessa** lä stooden'te'sä
student *(male)*	**lo studente** lo stooden'te
to study	**studiare** stoodyä're
to understand	**capire** käpē're
vacation	**la vacanza** lä väkän'tsä
to wait	**aspettare** äspetä're
wife	**la moglie** lä mo'lye
to write down	**scrivere** skrē'vere
yes	**sì** sē

28

BUSINESS CONTACTS

On the Phone

➡ see also: Communicating (p. 22)

This is *(name)*
atl*from (company)*.

Qui parla ... della ditta ...
kōō·ē' pär'lä ... de'lä dē'tä ...

I would like to speak
to ...

Vorrei parlare con ...
vōre'ē pärlä're kōn ...

❗ Sono io. sō'nō ē'ō.	Speaking.
❗ Glielo/Gliela passo. • lye'lō/lye'lä pä'sō.	I'll connect you.
❗ Attenda in linea, per favore. • äten'dä ēn lē'ne·ä, per fävō're.	Please hold.
❗ ... è occupato. • ... e ōkōōpä'tō.	... is busy at the moment.
❗ ... oggi non c'è. ... ō'jē nōn tshe.	... is not here today.
❓ Vuole lasciare detto qualcosa? • vōō·ō'le läshä're de'tō kōō·älkō'sä?	Would you like to leave a message?

May I leave a
message for ...?

Posso lasciare un messaggio per ...?
pō'sō läshä're ōōn mesä'jō per ...?

29

I'm here to see Mr. Rossi.	**Vorrei andare dal signor Rossi.** vōre'ē ändä're däl sēnyōr' rō'sē.
My name is ...	**Il mio nome è ...** ēl mē'ō nō'me e ...
I have an appointment with ... at ... o'clock.	**Ho un appuntamento con ... alle ...** ō ōōn äpōōntämen'tō kōn ... ä'le ...

! Un momento, per favore. ōōn mōmen'tō, per fävō're.	One moment, please.
! ... arriva subito. ... ärē'vä sōō'bētō.	... will be right here.
! ... è ancora ad una riunione. ... e änkō'rä äd ōō'nä rē-ōōnēō'ne.	... is still in a meeting.
! Venga, La accompagno da ... ven'gä, lä äkōmpä'nyō dä ...	Please follow me. I'll show you to ...
? Può attendere un istante, per favore? pōō-ō' äten'dere ōōn ēstän'te, per fävō're?	Would you please wait here a moment?

I'm looking for the ... booth.	**Cerco lo stand della ditta ...** tsher'kō lō ständ de'lä dē'tä ...
Do you have any brochures on ...?	**Ha del materiale informativo su ...?** ä del mäteryä'le ēnförmätē'vō sōō ...?

30

Do you also have pamphlets in English?	**Avete dei depliant anche in inglese?** ave'te de'ē deplē·än' än'ke ēn ēn·gle'se?
Whom can I ask?	**A chi mi posso rivolgere?** ä kē mē pō'sō rēvōl'jere.

Business Contacts

address	**l'indirizzo** lēndērē'tsō
to announce oneself	**annunciare** änōōntshyä're
appointment	**l'appuntamento** läpōōntämen'tō
auditorium	**il padiglione** ēl pädēlyō'ne
booth	**lo stand** lō ständ
to call (on the phone)	**telefonare** telefōnä're
catalog	**il catalogo** ēl kätä'lōgō
client, customer	**il cliente** ēl klē·en'te
company	**la ditta** lä dē'tä
conference	**la conferenza** lä kōnferen'tsä
– room	**la sala delle riunioni** lä sä'lä de'le rē·ōōnēō'nē
copy	**la fotocopia** lä fōtōkō'pyä
corporation	**il gruppo industriale** ēl grōō'pō ēndōōstrē·ä'le
department	**il reparto** ēl repär'tō
– head	**il direttore del reparto** ēl dēretō're del repär'tō

31

documents	**la documentazione**
	lä dōkōōmentätsyo'ne
entrance	**l'entrata** lentra'tä
exit	**l'uscita** lōōshe'tä
fax machine	**il telefax** ēl te'lefäks
information	**l'informazione** _f_ lēnfōrmätsyo'ne
interpreter	**l'interprete** _m, f_ lēnter'prete
management	**la direzione** lä dēretsyo'ne
manager	**il direttore** ēl dēreto're
to meet (up with someone)	**incontrare** ēnkōnträ're
meeting _(discussion)_	**la riunione** lä rē-ōōnyo'ne
meeting _(get-together)_	**l'incontro** lēnkōn'trō
news	**il messaggio** ēl mesä'jō
to notify	**avvisare** ävēsä're
office	**l'ufficio** lōōfē'tshō
price	**il prezzo** ēl pre'tsō
– list	**il listino prezzi** ēl lēstē'nō pre'tse
prospectus	**il depliant** ēl deplē-än'
reception	**la reception** lä resep'shōn
representative	**il rappresentante** ēl räpresentän'te
sample	**il campione** ēl kämpyo'ne
secretary	**la segretaria** lä segretär'yä
subsidiary	**la (società) filiale** lä (sōtshetä') fēlyä'le
telephone	**il telefono** ēl tele'fōnō
to telephone	**telefonare** telefōnä're
trade fair	**la fiera** lä fye'rä

32

Accommodations

INFORMATION

Where is the tourist information office?	**Dov'è l'ufficio informazioni turistiche?** dōve' lōōfē'tshō ēnförmätsyö'nē tōōrē'stēke?
Do you know where I can rent a room here?	**Mi saprebbe dire dove posso trovare una camera?** mē säpre'be dē're dō've pō'sō trōvä're ōō'nä kä'merä?

INFO The Tourist Information Office (**ufficio informazioni turistiche**) will be happy to give you information about hotels, guest houses, or rooms to rent in family homes.

Could you recommend ...	**Mi potrebbe consigliare ...** mē pōtre'be kōnsēlyä're ...
a good hotel?	**un buon albergo?** ōōn bōō·ōn' älber'gō?
an inexpensive hotel?	**un albergo economico?** ōōn älber'gō ekōnō'mēkō?
a boarding house?	**una pensione?** ōō'nä pensyō'ne?
a room at a private home?	**un alloggio presso privati?** ōōn älō'jō pre'sō prēvä'tē?
I'm looking for somewhere to stay ...	**Cerco un alloggio ...** tsher'kō ōōn älō'jō ...
in a *central/quiet* location.	**in *centro/una zona tranquilla.*** ēn tshen'trō/ōō'nä dzō'nä tränkōō·ē'lä.

34

at the beach.	**vicino alla spiaggia.** vētshē'nō ä'lä spyä'jä.
What will it cost (approximately)?	**Quanto costa (all'incirca)?** kōō·än'tō kō'stä (älēntshēr'kä)?
Can you make a reservation for me there?	**Mi può fare una prenotazione?** mē pōō·ō' fä're ōō'nä prenōtätsyō'ne?
Is there a *youth hostel/camping ground* here?	**C'è un ostello della gioventù/campeggio qui vicino?** tshe ōōn ōste'lō de'lä jōventōō'/kämpe'jō kōō·ē' vētshē'nō?
Is it far from here?	**È lontano da qui?** e lōntä'nō dä kōō·ē'?
How do I get there?	**Come ci si arriva?** kō'me tshē sē ärē'vä?
Can you draw me a map?	**Mi può fare uno schizzo della strada da fare?** mē pōō·ō' fä're ōō'nō skē'tsō de'lä strä'dä dä fä're?

HOTEL AND VACATION RENTAL

Hotel

I have a reservation. My name is …	**Ho una camera prenotata qui da voi. Il mio nome è …** ō ōō'nä kä'merä prenōtä'tä kōō·ē' dä voi. ēl mē'ō nō'me e …
Here is my confirmation.	**Ecco la conferma.** e'kō lä kōnfer'mä.

35

INFO If you would like a double room, you have a choice between a **camera matrimoniale** kä'merä mätrēmōnēä'le (a room with a double bed) and a **camera doppia** kä'merä dō'pyä (a room with two single beds).

Do you have a *double/single* room available …	**Avete una camera *doppia/singola* libera …** äve'te ōō'nä kä'merä dō'pyä/ sēn'gōlä lē'berä …
for *one night/ … nights?*	**per *una notte/… notti?*** per ōō'nä nō'te/… nō'tē?
with a *full bathroom/shower and toilet?*	**con *bagno/doccia e WC?*** kōn bä'nyō/dō'tshä e vōō-tshē'?
with a sea view?	**con vista sul mare?** kōn vē'stä sōōl mä're?
with a balcony?	**con balcone?** kōn bälkō'ne?

Purtroppo è tutto esaurito. pōōrtrō'pō e tōō'tō ezä-ōōrē'tō.	I'm sorry, but we're booked out.
Domani/Il … si libererà una camera. dōmä'nē/ēl … sē lēbererä' ōō'nä kä'merä.	Tomorrow/On … there will be a room available.

How much will it cost …	**Quanto costa …** kōō-än'tō kō'stä …
with/without breakfast?	**con/senza la prima colazione?** kōn/sen'tsä lä prē'mä kōlätsyō'ne?

36

with half board/full board included?	**a mezza pensione/pensione completa?** ä me'tsä pensyö'ne/ pensyö'ne kömple'tä?
Is there a discount for children?	**C'è una riduzione per i bambini?** tshe ōō'nä rēdōōtsyō'ne per ē bämbē'nē?
May I have a look at the room?	**Posso vedere la camera?** pō'sō vede're lä kä'merä?
Do you have a ... room?	**Avete una camera ...** äve'te ōō'nä kä'merä ...
less expensive	**più economica?** pyōō ekōnō'mēkä?
larger	**più grande?** pyōō grän'de?
quieter	**più tranquilla?** pyōō tränkōō-ē'lä?
It's very nice. I'll take it.	**È molto bella, la prendo.** e mōl'tō be'lä, lä pren'dō.

? Ha dei bagagli? ä de'ē bägä'lyē? Do you have any luggage?

Can you have a crib put in the room?	**Si può aggiungere un lettino per bambini?** sē pōō-o' äjōōn'jere ōōn letē'nō per bämbē'nē?
Where are the showers?	**Dove sono le docce?** dō've sō'nō le dō'tshe?
Where can I park my car?	**Dove posso mettere la macchina?** dō've pō'sō met'ere lä mä'kēnä?

Where is the *dining/ breakfast* room?	**Dov'è la sala *da pranzo/della prima colazione*?** döve´ lä sä´lä dä prän´tsö/ de´lä prē´mä kölätsyö´ne?
Can I have breakfast in my room?	**È possibile fare colazione in camera?** e pōse´bēle fä´re kölätsyö´ne en kä´merä?
Can I give you my valuables for safe-keeping?	**Le posso lasciare in custodia i miei oggetti di valore?** le pö´sö läshä´re ēn kōostö´dyä ē mye´ē öje´tē dē välö´re?
I'd like to pick up my valuables.	**Vorrei ritirare i miei oggetti di valore.** vōre´ē rētērä´re ē mye´ē öje´tē dē välö´re.
Can you exchange money for me?	**Mi potete cambiare dei soldi?** mē pöte´te kämbyä´re de´ē söl´dē?
I'd like the key to room …	**La chiave della camera …, per favore.** lä kyä´ve de´lä kä´merä …, per fävö´re.
Can I make a call to America (from my room)?	**Posso chiamare in America (dal telefono in camera)?** pö´sö kyämä´re ēn äme´rēkä (däl tele´fönö ēn kä´merä)?
Is there any mail/Are there any messages for me?	**C'è *posta/un messaggio* per me?** tshe pö´stä/ōōn mesä´jö per me?
I'd like a wakeup call at … o'clock (tomorrow morning), please.	**Per favore, mi svegli (domani mattina) alle …** per fävö´re, mē sve´lye (dömä´nē mätē´nä) ä´le …

| We're leaving tomorrow. | **Partiamo domattina.** |
| | pärtyä/mō dōmätë'nä. |

| Would you please prepare my bill? | **Prepari il conto, per favore.** |
| | prepä'rē ēl kōn'tō, per fävō're. |

| *I/We* really liked it here. | **È stato davvero piacevole qui.** |
| | e stä'tō däve'rō pyätshe'vōle kōō-ē'. |

| May I leave my luggage here until... o'clock? | **Posso lasciare qui i miei bagagli fino alle ...?** |
| | pō'sō läshä're kōō-ē' ē mye'ē bägä'lye fē'nō ä'le ...? |

2

| Would you call a taxi for me, please? | **Mi chiama un taxi, per favore?** |
| | mē kyä'mä ōōn tä'ksē, per fävō're? |

Vacation Rental

| We have rented the apartment ... | **Abbiamo preso in affitto l'appartamento ...** |
| | äbyä'mō pre'sō ēn äfē'tō läpärtämen'tō ... |

| Where can we pick up the keys to the apartment? | **Dove possiamo ritirare le chiavi dell'appartamento?** |
| | dō've pōsyä'mō rētērä're le kyä'vē deläpärtämen'tō? |

| Could you please explain how the ... works? | **Per favore, ci potrebbe spiegare come funziona ...** |
| | per fävō're, tshē pōtre'be spyegä're kō'me fōōntsyō'nä ... |

| stove | **la cucina elettrica?** |
| | lä kōōtshē'nä ele'trēkä? |

| dishwasher | **la lavastoviglie?** lä lävästōvē'lye? |

washing machine	**la lavatrice?** lä lävätrē'tshe?
Where do we put the trash?	**Dove si getta la spazzatura?** dō've sē je'tä lä spätsätōō'rä?
Where is the fuse box?	**Dove sono le valvole?** dō've sō'nō le väl'vōle?
Where is the meter?	**Dov'è il contatore?** dōve' ēl kōntätō're?
Where can I make a phone call?	**C'è un telefono qui?** tshe ōōn tele'fōnō kōō-ē'?
Can you please tell us where ... is?	**Ci saprebbe dire dov'è ...** tshē säpre'be dē're dōve' ...
a bakery	**una panetteria?** ōō'nä päneterē'ä?
the nearest bus stop	**la fermata dell'autobus più vicina?** lä fermä'tä delou'tōbōōs pyōō vētshē'nä?
a butcher	**una macelleria?** ōō'nä mätshelerē'ä?
a grocery store	**un negozio di alimentari?** ōōn negō'tsyō dē älēmentä'rē?

Complaints

see also Please; Thank you (p. 24)

The *shower/heating* doesn't work.	**La doccia/Il riscaldamento non funziona.** lä dō'tshä/ēl rēskäldämen'tō nōn fōōntsyō'nä.

The toilet doesn't flush.	**Lo sciacquone non funziona.**
	lō shäkōō·ō'ne nōn fōōntsyō'nä.
The window doesn't *open/close*.	**La finestra non si *apre/chiude*.**
	lä fēne'strä nōn sē ä'pre/kyōō'de.
Could I please have ...	**Per favore, potrei avere ancora ...**
	per fävō're, pōtre'ē äve're änkō'rä ...
another blanket?	**una coperta?** ōō'nä kōper'tä?
some more dish towels?	**degli strofinacci da cucina?**
	de'lyē strōfēnä'tshē dä kōōtshē'nä?
another towel?	**un asciugamano?**
	ōōn äshōōgämä'nō?
a few more clothes hangers?	**un paio di attaccapanni?**
	ōōn pä'yō dē ätäkäpä'nē?
The light doesn't work.	**La luce non funziona.**
	La lōō'tshe nōn fōōntsyō'nä.
There's no (hot) water.	**Non c'è acqua (calda).**
	nōn tshe ä'kōō·ä (käl'dä).
The drain/The toilet is stopped up.	**Il tubo di scarico/Il gabinetto è intasato.**
	ēl tōō'bō dē skä'rēkō/ēl gäbēne'tō e
	ēntäsä'tō.

2

Hotel and Vacation Rental

adapter	**il riduttore.** ēl rēdōōtō're
additional costs	**le spese di mantenimento** le spe'se dē
	mäntenēmen'tō
apartment	**l'appartamento** läpärtämen'tō
ashtray	**il posacenere** ēl pōsätshe'nere

41

balcony	**il balcone** ēl bälkō'ne
bathroom	**il bagno** ēl bä'nyō
bathtub	**la vasca da bagno** lä väs'kä dä bä'nyō
beach umbrella	**l'ombrellone** *m* lōmbrelō'ne
bed	**il letto** ēl le'tō
-side lamp	**la lampada del comodino** lä läm'pädä del kōmōdē'nō
bedspread	**il copriletto** ēl kōprēle'tō
bill	**il conto** ēl kōn'tō
blanket	**la coperta di lana** lä kōper'tä dē lä'nä
breakfast	**la colazione** lä kōlätsyō'ne
– buffet	**il buffet della colazione** ēl bōōfe' de'lä kōlätsyō'ne
broken	**rotto** rō'tō
broom	**la scopa** lä skō'pä
cabin	**il bungalow** ēl bōōn'gälō
chair	**la sedia** lä se'dyä
cleaning products	**il detersivo** ēl detersē'vō
closet	**l'armadietto** lärmädye'tō
complaint	**il reclamo** ēl reklä'mō
crib	**il lettino (per bambini)** ēl letē'nō (per bämbē'nē)
cup	**la tazza** lä tä'tsä
departure	**la partenza** lä pärten'tsä
dining room	**la sala da pranzo** lä sä'lä dä prän'tsō
dinner	**la cena** lä tshe'nä
dirty	**sporco** spōr'kō
dishes	**i piatti** ē pyä'tē
dishwasher	**la lavastoviglie** lä lävästōvē'lye

door	**la porta** lä pōr'tä
– lock	**la serratura** lä serätōō'rä
double room	**la camera doppia** lä kä'merä dō'pyä
electricity	**la corrente** lä kōren'te
elevator	**l'ascensore** *m* läshensō're
fan	**il ventilatore** ēl ventēlätō're
faucet	**il rubinetto (dell'acqua)**
	ēl rōōbēne'tō (delä'kōō·ä)
final cleaning	**la pulizia finale** lä pōōlētsē'ä fēnä'le
first floor	**il pianterreno** ēl pyäntere'nō
floor *(story)*	**il piano** ēl pyä'nō
flush	**lo sciacquone** lō shäkōō·ō'ne
full room and board	**la pensione completa**
	lä pensyō'ne kōmple'tä
fuse	**la valvola di sicurezza**
	lä väl'vōlä dē sēkōōre'tsä
gas cylinder	**la bombola del gas**
	lä bōm'bōlä del gäs
glass	**il bicchiere** ēl bēkye're
half room and board	**la mezza pensione** lä me'tsä pensyō'ne
high season	**l'alta stagione** läl'tä stäjō'ne
hotel	**l'hotel** *m,* **l'albergo** lōtel', lälber'gō
house	**la casa** lä kä'sä
key	**la chiave** lä kyä've
lamp	**la lampada** lä läm'pädä
light	**la luce** lä lōō'tshe
– bulb	**la lampadina** lä lämpädē'nä
– switch	**l'interruttore** *m* lēnterōōtō're

2

43

linens	**la biancheria da letto**
	lä byänkerē'ä dä le'tō
lost	**perso** per'sō
low season	**la fine stagione** lä fē'ne stäjō'ne
luggage	**i bagagli** ē bägä'lye
lunch	**il pranzo** ēl prän'tsō
maid	**la cameriera** lä kämerye'rä
mattress	**il materasso** ēl mäterä'sō
mirror	**lo specchio** lō spe'kyō
mosquito net	**la zanzariera** lä dzändzärye'rä
outlet	**la presa di corrente**
	lä pre'sä dē kōren'te
overnight stay	**il pernottamento** ēl pernōtämen'tō
pillow	**il cuscino** ēl kōōshē'nō
plate	**il piatto** ēl pyä'tō
plug	**la spina** lä spē'nä
pool	**la piscina** lä pēshē'nä
pre-season	**l'inizio stagione** *f* lēnē'tsyō stäjō'ne
reception	**la reception** lä resep'shōn
refrigerator	**il frigorifero** ēl frēgōrē'ferō
registration	**la registrazione** lä rejēsträtsyō'ne
rent	**l'affitto** läfē'tō
to rent	**prendere in affitto** pren'dere ēn äfē'tō
to reserve	**prenotare** prenōtä're
reserved	**prenotato** prenōtä'tō
room	**la camera** lä kä'merä
safe	**la cassaforte** lä käsäfōr'te
sheet	**il lenzuolo** ēl lentsōō-ō'lō
shower	**la doccia** lä dō'tshä

44

single room	**la camera singola** lä kä'merä sēn'gōlä
sink	**il lavandino** ēl lävändē'no
stairs	**la scala** lä skä'lä
table	**il tavolo** ēl tä'vōlō
tax on visitors	**la tassa di soggiorno** lä tä'sä dē sōjör'nō
telephone	**il telefono** ēl tele'fōnō
terrace	**la terrazza** lä terä'tsä
toilet	**il gabinetto** ēl gäbēne'tō
– paper	**la carta igienica** lä kär'tä ēje'nēkä
towel	**l'asciugamano** läshōōgämä'nō
trash container	**il bidone della spazzatura**
	ēl bēdō'ne de'lä spätsätōō'rä
trash can	**il secchio della spazzatura**
	ēl se'kyō de'lä spätsätōō'rä
TV room	**la sala della televisione**
	lä sä'lä de'lä televēzyō'ne
voltage	**il voltaggio** ēl vōltä'jo
to wake	**svegliare** svelyä're
water	**l'acqua** lä'kōō·ä
cold –	**l'acqua fredda** lä'kōō·ä fre'dä
hot –	**l'acqua calda** lä'kōō·ä käl'dä
window	**la finestra** lä fēne'strä
to work *(function)*	**funzionare** fōōntsyōnä're

2

45

YOUTH HOSTEL, CAMPING

Youth Hostel

Is there any room available?

C'è ancora un posto libero?
tshe änkō'rä ōōn pō'stō lē'berō?

I would like to stay for *one night/... nights.*

Vorrei rimanere per *una notte/... notti.*
vōre'ē rēmäne're per ōō'nä nō'te/... nō'tē.

How much will it cost for one night (per person)?

Quanto costa il pernottamento (a persona)? kōō·än'tō kō'stä ēl pernōttämen'tō (ä persō'nä)?

Do you also have double rooms?

Avete anche delle camere doppie?
äve'te än'ke de'le kä'mere dō'pye?

Is breakfast included?

È compresa la prima colazione?
e kōmpre'sä lä prē'mä kōlätsyō'ne?

How much does ... cost?

Quanto costa ... kōō·än'tō kō'stä ...

breakfast

la prima colazione?
lä prē'mä kōlätsyō'ne?

lunch
dinner

il pranzo? ēl prän'tsō?
la cena? lä tshe'nä?

Where is the dining room?

Dov'è la sala da pranzo?
dōve' lä sä'lä dä prän'tsō

When are the meals served?

A che ora si mangia?
ä ke ō'rä sē män'jä?

Where can I buy something *to eat/ to drink*?	**Dov'è che si può comprare qualcosa da** ***mangiare/bere?*** dōve' ke sē pōō-ō' kömprä're kōō-älkô'sä dä mänjä're/be're?
Where are the bathrooms?	**Dove sono i bagni?** dō've sō'nō ē bä'nye?
Where are the restrooms?	**Dove sono i gabinetti?** dō've sō'nō ē gäbēne'tē?
Can I do some laundry here?	**Si può lavare la propria biancheria qui?** sē pōō-ō' lävä're lä prō'prē-ä byänkerē'ä kōō-ē'?
Do you have any lockers?	**Ci sono delle cassette di sicurezza?** tshē sō'nō de'le käse'te dē sēkōōre'tsä?
When do I have to be back by?	**Fino a che ora si può rientrare la sera?** fē'nō ä ke ō'rä sē pōō-ō' rē-enträ're lä se'rä?
How can I get to the middle of town?	**Come si arriva in centro?** kō'me sē ärē'vä ēn tshen'trō?
Where's the nearest bus stop?	**Dov'è la fermata dell'autobus più vicina?** dōve' lä fermä'tä delou'tōbōōs pyōō vētshē'nä?

Camping

May we camp on your property?	**Possiamo campeggiare sul vostro terreno?** pōsyä'mō kämpejä're sōōl vōs'trō tere'nō?

2

Do you still have room for ...?	**Ci sono ancora posti per ...?** tshē sō'nō änkō'rä pō'stē per ...?
What is the charge for ...	**Quanto si paga per ...** kōō·än'tō sē pä'gä per ...
... adults and ... children?	**... adulti e ... bambini?** ... ädōōl'tē e ... bämbē'nē?
a car with a trailer?	**una macchina con roulotte?** ōō'nä mä'kēnä kōn rōōlōt'?
a camping van?	**un camper?** ōōn käm'per?
a tent?	**una tenda?** ōō'nä ten'dä?
Do you also rent *cabins/camping trailers*?	**Affittate anche *bungalows/roulotte*?** äfētä'te än'ke *bōōn'gälōs/rōōlōt'*?
We'd like a place in the shade.	**Vorremmo un posto all'ombra.** vōre'mō ōōn pō'stō älōm'brä.
We'd like to stay for one *night/... nights*.	**Vorremmo rimanere per *una notte/ ... notti*.** vōre'mō rēmäne're per *ōō'nä nō'te/... nō'tē*.
Where can we *pitch our tent/park our van*?	**Dove possiamo *piantare la tenda/ parcheggiare la roulotte*?** dō've pōsyä'mō *pyäntä're lä ten'dä/pärkejä're lä rōōlōt*?
Where are the bathrooms?	**Dove sono i bagni?** dō've sō'nō ē bä'nyē?

48

Where are the rest rooms?	**Dove sono i gabinetti?** dō've sō'nō ē gäbēne'tē?
Is there a power outlet here?	**C'è una presa di corrente qui?** tshe ōō'nä pre'sä dē kōren'te kōō-ē'?
Where can I ...	**Dove si può ...** dō've sē pōō-ō' ...
empty the chemical waste from the toilet?	**svuotare il WC chimico?** svōō-ōtä're ēl vōō-tshe' kē'mēkō?
empty sewage water?	**versare l'acqua di scarico?** versä're lä'kōō-ä dē skä'rēko?
fill the tank with fresh water?	**fare rifornimento di acqua?** fä're rēfōrnēmen'tō dē ä'kōō-ä?
Does the hot shower cost extra?	**Bisogna pagare extra per la doccia calda?** bēzō'nyä pägä're ek'strä per lä dō'tshä käl'dä?
Is there a grocery store here?	**C'è un negozio di alimentari qui?** tshe ōōn negō'tsyō dē älēmentä'rē kōō-ē'?
Can I *rent/exchange* gas cylinders here?	**Dove si *comprano/cambiano* le bombole del gas qui?** dō've sē *kōm'pränō/käm'byänō* le bōm'bōle del gäs kōō-ē'?
May I borrow a(n) ..., please?	**Per favore, mi potrebbe prestare ...?** per fävō're, mē pōtre'be prestä're ...?

air mattress	**il materassino gonfiabile**
	ēl mäteräsē'nō gōnfyä'bēle
bathrooms	**i bagni** ē bä'nyē
bed linens	**la biancheria (da letto)**
	lä byänkerē'ä (dä le'tō)
breakfast	**la prima colazione** lä prē'mä kōlätsyō'ne
cabin	**il bungalow** ēl bōōn·gälō
to camp, to go camping	**campeggiare** kämpejä're
camping	**il campeggio** ēl kämpe'jō
– permit	**la tessera di campeggio**
	lä te'serä dē kämpe'jō
– trailer	**la roulotte** lä rōōlōt'
– van	**il camper** ēl käm'per
campsite	**il campeggio** ēl kämpe'jō
candle	**la candela** lä kän'delä
check-in	**la registrazione** lä rejēsträtsyō'ne
chemical toilet *(in a van)*	**il WC chimico** ēl vōō-tshē' kē'mēkō
communal room	**la sala di soggiorno** lä sä'lä dē sōjōr'nō
to cook	**cucinare** kōōtshēnä're
detergent	**il detersivo** ēl detersē'vō
dining room	**la sala da pranzo** lä sä'lä dä prän'tsō
dinner	**la cena** lä tshe'nä
dormitory	**il dormitorio**
	ēl dōrmētōr'yō
double room	**la camera doppia** lä kä'merä dō'pyä

drier *(clothes)*	**l'asciugabiancheria** läshōōgäbyänkerē'ä
drinking water	**l'acqua potabile** lä'kōō·ä potä'bēle
electricity	**la corrente** lä kōren'te
to fill (up)	**riempire** rē·empē're
foam (insulation) mat	**la stuoia isolante** lä stōō·ō'yä ēsōlän'te
gas canister	**la cartuccia del gas** lä kärtōō'tshä del gäs
gas cylinder	**la bombola del gas** lä bōm'bōlä del gäs
gas lantern	**la lampada a gas** lä läm'pädä ä gäs
group of kids	**il gruppo giovanile** ēl grōō'pō jōvänē'le
hammer	**il martello** ēl märte'lō
hostel father	**il papà albergatore** ēl päpä' älbergätō're
hostel mother	**la mamma albergatrice** lä mä'mä älbergätrē'tshe
to iron	**stirare** stērä're
locker	**la cassetta di sicurezza** lä käse'tä dē sēkōōre'tsä
lunch	**il pranzo** ēl prän'tsō
membership card	**la tessera di membro** lä te'serä dē mem'brō
mosquito net	**la zanzariera** lä dzändzärēe'ra
mosquito repellant	**il fornellino antizanzare** ēl fōrnelē'nō äntēdzän'dzäre
outlet	**la presa di corrente** lä pre'sä dē kōren'te
overnight stay	**il pernottamento** ēl pernōtämen'tō
to set up	**piantare** pyäntä're
plates	**i piatti** ē pyä'tē

playground	**il campo da gioco** ēl käm'pō dä jō'kō
plug	**la spina** lä spē'nä
pot	**la pentola** lä pen'tōlä
to rent	**noleggiare** nōlejä're
rental fee	**la tariffa di noleggio** lä tärē'fä dē nōle'jō
room	**la camera** lä kä'merä
shower	**la doccia** lä dō'tshä
to take a shower	**fare la doccia** fä're lä dō'tshä
site	**il posto** ēl pō'stō
sleeping bag	**il sacco a pelo** ēl sä'kō ä pe'lō
stove *(camping)*	**il fornello** ēl fōrne'lō
tent	**la tenda** lä ten'dä
– peg	**il picchetto** ēl pēke'tō
toilet	**il gabinetto** ēl gäbēne'tō
usage fee	**la tariffa per l'uso** lä tärē'fä per lōō'zō
to wash	**lavare** lävä're
washing machine	**la lavatrice** lä lävätrē'tshe
water canister	**la tanica per l'acqua** lä tä'nēkä per lä'kōō·ä
youth hostel	**l'ostello della gioventù** lōste'lō de'lä jōventōō'
youth hostel card	**la tessera per gli ostelli della gioventù** lä te'serä per lyē ōste'lē de'lä jōventōō'

52

On the Way

ASKING THE WAY

Excuse me, where is …?	**Scusi, dov'è …?** skōō'zē, dōve' …
How can I get to …?	**Come si arriva a …?** kō'me sē ärē'vä ä … ?

What's the *quickest*/
cheapest way to get to
the …

Come si arriva nel modo più *veloce*/
***economico* …** kō'me sē ärē'vä nel mō'dō
pyōō velō'tshe/ekōnō'mēkō …

train station?	**alla stazione?** ä'lä stätsyō'ne?
bus station?	**alla stazione dei pullman?** ä'lä stätsyō'ne de'ē pōōl'män?
airport?	**all'aeroporto?** älä-erōpōr'tō?
harbor?	**al porto?** äl pōr'tō?

! **Il modo migliore è con il taxi.**
• ēl mō'dō mēlyō're e kōn ēl tä'ksē.

The best thing to do
is take a taxi.

| How do I get to the interstate highway? | **Come si arriva all'autostrada?** kō'me sē ärē'vä äloutōsträ'dä? |

! **Mi dispiace, non lo so.**
• mē dēspyä'tshe, nōn lō sō.

I'm afraid I don't
know.

! **Là.** lä.

Over there.

! **Indietro.** ēndye'trō.

Go back.

! **Sempre diritto.** sem'pre dērē'tō.

Straight ahead.

!	**A destra.** ä de'strä.	To the right.
!	**A sinistra.** ä sēnē'strä.	To the left.
!	**La *prima/seconda* strada a *sinistra/destra.*** lä prē'mä/sekōn'dä strä'dä ä sēnē'strä/de'strä.	The *first/second* street to the *left/ right.*
!	**Al semaforo.** äl semä'fōrō.	At the traffic lights.
!	**Dopo l'incrocio.** dō'pō lēnkrō'tshō.	After the intersection.
	Attraversi … äträver'sē …	Cross …
!	**il ponte!** ēl pōn'te.	the bridge.
	la piazza! lä pyä'tsä.	the square.
	la strada! lä strä'dä.	the street.
!	**Poi chieda a qualcun altro.** poi kye'dä ä kōō-älkōōn' äl'trō.	Then ask again.
	Può prendere … pōō-ō' pren'dere …	You can take …
!	**l'autobus.** lou'tōbōōs	the bus.
	il tram. ēl träm.	the streetcar.
	la metropolitana. lä metrōpōlētä'nä	the subway.

Is this the road to …?	**È questa la strada per …?** e kōō·e'stä lä strä'dä per …?

3

55

| How far is it? | **Quant'è lontano?** kōō·änte' lōntä'nō? | |

| ! | **Abbastanza lontano.**
äbästän'tsä lōntä'nō. | Pretty far. |

| ! | **Non è lontano.** nōn e lōntä'nō. | Not (very) far. |

| ! | **È qui vicino.** e kōō·ē vētshē'nō. | It's very close. |

| How many minutes
on foot/by car? | **Quanti minuti ci vogliono** *a piedi/con la*
***macchina*?** kōō·än'tē mēnōō'tē tshē vō-
lyō'nō *ä pye'dē/kōn lä mä/kēnä*? | |

| Could you show me
on the map? | **Me lo può indicare sulla cartina, per**
favore? me lō pōō·ō' ēndēkä're sōō'lä
kärtē'nä, per fävō're? | |

AT THE BORDER

Passport Control

| ! | **I (Suoi) documenti, per favore.**
ē (sōō·oi') dōkōōmen'tē,
per fävō're. | May I see your
documents, please? |

| ! | **Il Suo passaporto, per favore.**
ēl sōō'ō päsäpōr'tō, per fävō're. | May I see your
passport, please? |

| ! | **Il Suo passaporto è scaduto.**
ēl sōō'ō päsäpōr'tō e skädōō'tō. | Your passport is
expired. |

| I'm with the ... group. | **Faccio parte della comitiva ...** fä'tshō pär'te de'lä kōmētē'vä ... | |

Customs

?	**Ha qualcosa da dichiarare?** ä kōō-älkō'sä dä dēkyärä're?	Do you have anything to declare?
!	**Apra** *il portabagagli/la valigia,* **per favore.** ä'prä *ēl pōrtäbägä'lyē/ lä väle'jä,* per fävō're.	Open the *trunk/ suitcase,* please.
!	**Deve sdoganare questo.** de've zdōgänä're kōō-e'stō.	You have to declare that.

At the Border

bill	**la fattura** lä fätōō'rä
border	**la frontiera** lä frōntye'rä
car registration	**i documenti dell'autoveicolo** e dōkōōmen'tē deloutōve-ē'kōlō
country identi- fication sticker	**la targa di nazionalità** lä tär'gä dē nätsyōnälētä'
customs – declaration	**la dogana** lä dōgä'nä **la dichiarazione doganale** lä dēkyärätsyō'ne dōgänä'le
date	**la data** lä dä'tä
documents	**i documenti** ē dōkōōmen'tē
driver's license	**la patente (di guida)** lä päten'te (dē gōō-ē'dä)
expired	**scaduto** skädōō'tō

57

first name	**il nome** ēl nō'me
identity	**la carta d'identità** lä kär'tä dēdentētä'
invalid	**non valido** nōn vä'lēdō
last name	**il cognome** ēl kōnyō'me
nationality	**la nazionalità** lä nätsyōnälētä'
passport	**il passaporto** ēl päsäpōr'tō
– control	**il controllo dei passaporti**
	ēl kōntrō'lō de'ē päsäpōr'tē
residence	**la residenza** lä rezēden'tsä
(permanent)	
residence	**il domicilio** ēl dōmētshē'lyō
(temporary)	
to renew	**prolungare** prōlōōn·gä're
travel group	**la comitiva turistica**
	lä kōmētē'vä tōōrē'stēkä
VAT	**l'IVA (imposta sul valore aggiunto)**
	lēvä' (ēmpō'stä sōōl välō're äjōōn'tō)

LUGGAGE

May I *leave/pick up* my luggage here?	**Vorrei *depositare/ritirare* i miei bagagli.** vôre'ē *depôsētä're/rētērä're* ē mye'ē bägä'lyē.
May I leave my backpack with you *for an hour/until …*?	**Potrei lasciare qui il mio zaino *per un'ora/fino a …*?** pôtre'ē läshä're kōō-ē' ēl mē'ō dzī'nō *per ōōnō'rä/fē'nō ä …*?
I'd like to have these bags sent to …	**Vorrei spedire questo bagaglio per …** vôre'ē spedē're kōō-e'stō bägä'lyō per …
When will they be at …?	**Quando arriverà a …?** kōō-än'dō ärēverä' ä …?
My luggage hasn't arrived (yet).	**I miei bagagli non sono (ancora) arrivati.** ē mye'ē bägä'lyē nōn sō'nō (änkō'rä) ärēvä'tē.
Where is my luggage?	**Dove sono i miei bagagli?** dō've sō'nō ē mye'ē bägä'lyē?
Those aren't my things.	**Queste non sono le mie cose.** kōō-e'ste nōn sō'nō le mē'e kō'se.
A suitcase is missing.	**Manca una valigia.** män'kä ōō'nä välē'jä.
My luggage has been damaged.	**La mia valigia è stata danneggiata.** lä mē'ä välē'jä e stä'tä dänejä'tä.
Who can I report it to?	**A chi mi posso rivolgere?** ä kē'mē pô'sō rēvôl'jere?

3

59

backpack	**lo zaino** lō dzī'nō
bag	**la borsa** lä bōr'sä
baggage	**il bagaglio** ēl bägä'lyō
– check-in	**l'accettazione *f* bagagli** lätshetätsyō'ne bägä'lyē
– claim	**la riconsegna bagagli** lä rēkōnse'nyä bägä'lyē
– storage	**il deposito bagagli** ēl depō'sētō bägä'lyē
– ticket	**lo scontrino dei bagagli** lō skōntrē'nō de'ē bägä'lyē
carry-on baggage	**il bagaglio a mano** ēl bägä'lyō ä mä'nō
to check in	**depositare** depōsētä're
(baggage)	
excess baggage	**l'eccesso di bagaglio** letshe'sō dē bägä'lyō
flight bag	**la borsa da viaggio** lä bōr'sä dä vyä'jō
to leave here	**lasciare qui** läshä're kōō·ē'
locker	**il deposito bagagli a cassette** ēl depō'sētō bägä'lyē ä käse'te
to pick up	**ritirare** rētērä're
suitcase	**la valigia** lä välē'jä

PLANE

Information and Booking

Where is the ... counter?	**Dov'è lo sportello della ... ?** dōve' lō spōrte'-lō de'lä ... ?
When is the next flight to ...?	**Quando parte il prossimo aereo per ...?** kōō-än'dō pär'te ēl prō'sēmō ä-e're-ō per ...?
When will a plane be flying to ... *today/tomorrow*?	**Quando parte *oggi/domani* un aereo per ... ?** kōō-än'dō pär'te ō'jē/dōmä'nē ōōn ä-e're-ō per ...?
When will we be in ...?	**Quando arriviamo a ... ?** kōō-än'dō ärēvyä'mō ä ... ?
How much will it cost to fly to ... (round-trip)?	**Quanto costa un volo (di andata e ritorno) per ... ?** kōō-än'tō kō'stä ōōn vō'lō (dē ändä'tä e rētōr'nō) per ...?
I'd like a ... ticket to ..., please.	**Un biglietto per ..., per favore, ...** ōōn bēlye'tō per ..., per fävō're.
one-way.	**di sola andata.** dē sō'lä ändä'tä.
round-trip.	**di andata e ritorno.** dē ändä'tä e rētōr'nō.
economy class.	**di classe turistica.** dē klä'se tōōrē'stēkä.
business class.	**di business class.** dē bēz'nes kläs.
first-class.	**di prima classe.** dē prē'mä klä'se.

| ! | **Purtroppo su questo volo non ci** **sono più posti.** pōōrtrō′pō sōō kōō·e′stō vō′lō nōn tshē sō′nō pyōō pō′stē. | I'm afraid this flight is booked out. |

Are there any *special rates/stand-by seats* available? — **Ci sono *tariffe speciali/posti stand-by*?** tshē sō′nō tärē′fe spetsh·ä′lē/pō′stē ständ′bī′?

I'd like ... — **Vorrei un posto ...** vōre′ē ōōn pō′stō ...

a window seat. — **accanto al finestrino.** äkän′tō äl fēnestrē′nō.

an aisle seat. — **accanto al corridoio.** äkän′tō äl kōrēdoi′ō.

a seat in non-smoking. — **per non fumatori.** per nōn fōōmätō′rē.

a seat in smoking. — **per fumatori.** per fōōmätō′rē.

Where is Gate B? — **Dov'è l'uscita B?** dōve′ lōōshē′tä bē?

How late is the flight to ... ? — **Quanto ritardo ha l'aereo per ...?** kōō·än′tō rētär′dō ä lä·e′re·ō per ...?

I'd like to *confirm/cancel* my flight. — **Vorrei *confermare/annullare* questo volo.** vōre′ē kōnfermä′re/änōōlä′re kōō·e′stō vō′lō.

I'd like to change my flight. — **Vorrei cambiare la data del biglietto.** vōre′ē kämbyä′re lä dä′tä del bēlyē′tō.

On the Plane

Could I have *(another/some more)* …, please?	**Per favore, potrei avere (ancora) … ?** per fävo´re, pōtre´ē äve´re (änkō´rä) …?
I feel sick.	**Mi sento male.** mē sen´tō mä´le.
When do we land?	**Quando atterriamo?** kōō·än´dō äteryä´mō?

Plane

airline	**la compagnia aerea** lä kōmpänyē´ä ä·e´re·ä
airplane	**l'aereo** lä·e´re·ō
airport	**l'aeroporto** lä·erōpôr´tō
– tax	**la tassa aeroportuale** lä täs´sä ä·erōpōrtōō·ä´le
airsickness	**il mal d'aria** ēl mäl d'ä´ryä
arrival	**l'arrivo** lärē´vō
to book	**prenotare** prenōtä´re
to cancel	**annullare** änōōlä´re
to change a flight	**cambiare la data del biglietto** kämbyä´re lä dä´tä del bēlye´tō
charter flight	**il volo charter** ēl vō´lō tshär´ter
class	**la classe** lä klä´se
to confirm	**confermare** kōnfermä´re
counter	**lo sportello** lō spōrte´lō
delay	**il ritardo** ēl rētär´dō
departure	**il decollo** ēl dekō´lō

3

63

exit	**l'uscita** lo͞oshē'tä
flight	**il volo** ēl vō'lō
– attendant *(female)*	**l'hostess** *f* lōs'tes
– attendant *(male)*	**lo steward** *m* lō styo͞o'ärd
return –	**il volo di ritorno** ēl vō'lō dē rētōr'nō
scheduled –	**il volo di linea** ēl vō'lō dē lē'ne·ä
to fly	**andare in aereo** ändä're ēn ä·e're·ō
hand baggage	**il bagaglio a mano** ēl bägä'lyō ä mä'nō
information desk	**l'ufficio informazioni** lo͞ofē'tshō ēnfōrmätsyō'ne
to land	**atterrare** äterä're
local time	**l'ora locale** lō'rä lōkä'le
nonsmoker	**non fumatori** *m/pl* nōn fo͞omätō're
smoker	**fumatori** *m/pl* fo͞omätō're
stopover	**lo scalo** lō skä'lō
to take off	**decollare** dekōlä're
ticket	**il biglietto** ēl bēlye'tō

RAIL

Information and Tickets

Where is the *train/ tourist* information office?

Dov'è l'ufficio *informazioni/turistico*? dōve' lo͞ofē'tshō ēnfōrmätsyō'ne/ to͞ore'stekō?

Where can I find the *baggage storage/ lockers*?

Dov'è il *deposito bagagli/deposito bagagli a cassette*? dōve' ēl depō'sētō bägä'lyē/depō'sētō bägä'lyē ä käse'te?

64

INFO It is more common to travel by train in Italy than in the United States. A normal second-class ticket does not include a seat reservation; you may choose from whichever seats are not taken. You have a choice of trains between the **rapidi** rä'pēdē (express trains that stop only at cities) and the **espressi** espre'sē (local trains that stop more frequently). Recently a third option has been added: the **treni ad alta velocità** tre'nē äd äl'tä velōtshētä' (high-speed trains), for which you must pay extra and are required to reserve a seat. Some of these trains only have first-class cars. No matter which train you take, it would be a good idea to reserve a seat since the trains are often very full. You can make your reservations up to an hour before departure.

When is the *next/last* train to …?	**Quando parte *il prossimo/l'ultimo* treno per …?** kōō·än'dō pär'te ēl prō'sēmō/ lōōl'tēmō tre'nō per …?
When will it arrive in …?	**Quando arriva a …?** kōō·än'dō äre'vä ä …?
When are the trains to …?	**Che treni ci sono per …?** ke tre'nē tshē sō'nō per …?
Do I have to change trains?	**Devo cambiare?** de'vō kämbyä're?
Which platform does the train to … leave from?	**Da quale binario parte il treno per …?** dä kōō·ä'le bēnär'yō pär'te ēl tre'nō per …?

How much does a ticket to … cost?	**Quanto costa il biglietto per … ?**
	kōō·än'tō kō'stä ēl bēlye'tō per …?
Are there special rates for …?	**C'è una riduzione per …?**
	tshe ōō'nä rēdōōtsēō'ne per …?
Do you have to pay extra for this train?	**Per questo treno ci vuole il supplemento?** per kōō·e'stō tre'nō tshē vōō·o'le ēl sōōplemen'tō?
I'd like *a … ticket/ two … tickets* to …, please.	*Un biglietto/Due biglietti* per …, **per favore, …** ōōn bēlye'tō/dōō'e bēlye'tē per …, per fävō're, …
one-way	**di sola andata.** dē sō'lä ändä'tä.
round-trip	**di andata e ritorno.** dē ändä'tä e rētōr'nō.
first/second class	**di *prima/seconda* classe.** dē prē'mä/sekōn'dä klä'se.
for children.	**per bambini.** per bämbē'nē.

INFO If you have a round-trip ticket, you must get it stamped before you begin the return portion of your trip. There are special machines at the train station for this purpose.

| I'd like to reserve a seat on the … o'clock train to …, please. | **Vorrei prenotare un posto sul treno delle … per …, per favore.** vōre'ē prenōtä're ōōn pō'stō sōōl tre'nō de'le … per …, per fävo're. |

I'd like a seat …	**Vorrei un posto** … vōre'ē ōōn pō'stō …
by the window.	**accanto al finestrino.**
	äkän'tō äl fēnestrē'nō.
in nonsmoking.	**per non fumatori.**
	per nōn fōōmätō'rē.
in smoking.	**per fumatori.** per fōōmätō'rē.
I'd like to bring a bicycle with me.	**Vorrei portarmi dietro la bicicletta.**
	vōre'ē pōrtär'mē dye'trō lä bētshēkle'tä.

Information

Accettazione bagagli ätshetätsyō'ne bägä'lyē	Baggage Check-In
Ai binari ī bēnä'rē	To All Trains
Binario bēnär'yō	Track
Deposito bagagli depō'sētō bägä'lyē	Baggage Storage
Deposito bagagli a cassette depō'sētō bägä'lyē ä käse'te	Lockers
Gabinetti gäbēne'tē	Rest Rooms
Informazioni ēnfōrmätsyō'nē	Information
Ristorante rēstōrän'te	Restaurant
Sala d'aspetto sä'lä däspe'tō	Waiting Room
Uscita ōōshē'tä	Exit

3

67

On the Train

May I sit here?	**È libero questo posto?** e lē'berō kōō·e'stō pō'stō?
Excuse me, but I believe this is my seat.	**Scusi, ma questo è il mio posto.** skōō'zē, mä kōō·e'stō e ēl mē'ō pō'stō.
Would you mind if I *opened/closed* the window?	**Posso *aprire/chiudere* il finestrino?** pō'sō äprē're/kyōō'dere ēl fēnestrē'nō?

! **I biglietti, prego!** ē bēlye'tē, pre'gō!   Tickets, please!

How many more stops to …?	**Quante stazioni ci sono ancora prima di …?** kōō·än'te stätsyō'nē tshē sō'nō änkō'rä prē'mä dē …?
How long is our layover?	**Quanto tempo si ferma il treno?** kōō·än'tō tem'pō sē fer'mä ēl tre'nō?
Will I be in time to catch the train to …?	**Faccio ancora in tempo a prendere il treno per …?** fä'tshō änkō'rä ēn tem'pō ä pren'dere ēl tre'nō per …?

Train

to arrive	**arrivare** ärēvä're
car	**il vagone** ēl vägō'ne
to change (trains)	**cambiare** kämbyä're
class	**la classe** lä klä'se
compartment	**lo scompartimento** lō skōmpärtēmen'tō
connection	**la coincidenza** lä kō·ēntshēden'tsä

to depart	**partire** pärtē´re
dining car	**il vagone ristorante**
	ēl vägō´ne rēstörän´te
discount	**la riduzione** lä rēdōōtsyō´ne
exit	**l'uscita** lōōshē´tä
extra cost	**il supplemento** ēl sōōplemen´tō
to get off	**scendere** shen´dere
to get on	**salire** sälē´re
to go by train	**andare in treno** ändä´re ēn tre´nō
fare	**il prezzo del biglietto**
	ēl pre´tsō del bēlye´tō
lockers	**il deposito bagagli a cassette**
	ēl depō´sētō bägä´lyē ä käse´te
platform	**il binario** ēl bēnär´yō
reserved	**prenotato** prenōtä´tō
seat	**il posto** ēl pō´stō
sleeping car	**il vagone letto** ēl vägō´ne le´tō
(1–4 beds)	
sleeping car	**la carrozza con cuccette**
(many beds)	lä kärō´tsä kōn kōōtshe´te
stop	**la fermata** lä fermä´tä
occupied	**occupato** ōkōōpä´tō
through car	**la carrozza diretta** lä kärō´tsä dēre´tä
ticket	**il biglietto** ēl bēlye´tō
timetable	**l'orario** lōrär´yō
track	**il binario** ēl bēnär´yō
train	**il treno** ēl tre´nō
– station	**la stazione** lä stätsyō´ne

BOAT

Information and Booking

When will there
be a *ship/ferry* going
to ...?

Quando parte *una nave/un traghetto*
per ...? kōō·än'dō pär'te ōō'nä nä've/
ōōn träge'tō per ...)

How long is the
passage to ...?

Quanto dura la traversata fino a ...?
kōō·än'tō dōō'rä lä träversä'tä fē'nō ä ...?

At which *ports/islands*
will we be landing?

Quali *porti/isole* si toccano?
kōō·ä'lē *pōr'tē/ē'zōle* sē tōkä'nō?

When do we land?

Quando sbarchiamo a ...?
kōō·än'dō zbärkyä'mō ä ...?

When must we be on
board?

Quando dobbiamo essere a bordo?
kōō·än'dō dōbyä'mō e'sere ä bōr'dō?

I'd like to board with
a car.

Vorrei imbarcare la macchina.
vōre'ē ēmbärkä're lä mä'kēnä.

I'd like a *first
class/tourist class*
ticket to ...

Vorrei un biglietto di *prima classe/*
classe turistica* per ... vōre'ē ōōn
bēlye'tō dē *prē'mä klä'se/klä'se*
tōōrē'stēkä per ...

I'd like a single cabin.

Vorrei una cabina singola.
vōre'ē ōō'nä käbē'nä sēn'gōla.

I'd like a ticket for
the excursion at ...
o'clock.

Vorrei un biglietto per il giro delle ...
vōre'ē ōōn bēlye'tō per ēl jē'rō de'le ...

| Where has the ... docked? | **Dov'è approdata la ... ?** |
| | dōve' äprōdä'tä lä ...? |

On Board

| I'm looking for cabin number ... | **Cerco la cabina numero ...** |
| | tsher'ko lä kä'bēnä nōō'merō ... |

| May I have a different cabin? | **Potrei avere un'altra cabina?** |
| | pōtre'ē äve're ōōnäl'trä käbē'nä? |

| Do you have something for seasickness? | **Ha qualcosa contro il mal di mare?** |
| | ä kōō-äl'kō'sa kōn'trō ēl mäl dē mä're? |

Boat

3

air conditioning	**l'impianto dell'aria condizionata**
	lēmpyän'tō delär'yä kōndētsyōnä'tä
blanket	**la coperta di lana** lä kōper'tä dē lä'nä
boat trip	**la crociera** lä krōtshe'rä
cabin	**la cabina** lä käbē'nä
double –	**la cabina doppia** lä käbē'nä dō'pyä
exterior –	**la cabina esterna** lä käbē'nä ester'nä
four-bed –	**la cabina a quattro posti**
	lä käbē'nä ä kōō-ä'trō pō'stē
interior –	**la cabina interna** lä käbē'nä ēnter'nä
single –	**la cabina singola** lä käbē'nä sēn'gōlä
canal	**il canale** ēl känä'le
captain	**il capitano** ēl käpētä'nō
car ferry	**la nave traghetto** lä nä've träge'tō
coast	**la costa** lä kō'stä

71

deck	**la coperta** lä kōper'tä
duty	**i diritti portuali** ē dērē'tē pōrtōō-ä'lē
duty-free store	**il duty-free-shop** ēl dēōō'tē-frē-shōp'
excursion	**la gita** lä jē'tä
ferry	**il traghetto** ēl träge'tō
hovercraft	**l'hoverkraft** *m* lō'verkräft
island	**l'isola** lē'zōlä
land excursion	**la gita a terra** lä jē'tä ä te'rä
landing	**l'approdo** läprō'dō
life boat	**la scialuppa di salvataggio** lä shälōō'pä dē sälvätä'jō
life vest	**il giubbotto di salvataggio** ēl jōōbō'tō dē sälvätä'jō
lounge chair	**la sedia a sdraio** lä se'dyä ä zdrī'ō
passage	**la traversata** lä träversä'tä
port *(harbor)*	**il porto** ēl pōr'tō
port *(side of boat)*	**a babordo** ä bäbōr'dō
rough sea	**il mare mosso** ēl mä're mō'sō
sea	**il mare** ēl mä're
– sickness	**il mal di mare** ēl mäl dē mä're
ship	**la nave** lä nä've
ship's agent	**l'agenzia navale** läjen'tsyä nävä'le
shore	**la riva** lä rē'vä
starboard	**a dritta** ä drē'tä
steward	**il cameriere** ēl kämerye're
sun deck	**il ponte di passeggiata** ēl pōn'te dē päsejä'tä
swimming pool	**la piscina** lä pēshē'nä

72

CAR, MOTORBIKE AND BIKE

Rentals

I'd like to rent a …
(with automatic
transmission).

Vorrei noleggiare … (con il cambio automatico). vōrè'ē nōlejä're … (kōn ēl käm'byō outōmä'tēkō).

   car

   car with four-
   wheel drive

   motorcycle

una macchina ōō'nä mä'kēnä

un fuoristrada ōōn fōō·ōrēsträ'dä

una motocicletta
ōō'nä mōtōtshēkle'tä

   motor home

un camper ōōn käm'per

? **Mi fa vedere la Sua patente, per favore?** mē fä vede're lä sōō'ä päten'te, per fävō're?

May I see your
driver's license,
please?

3

I'd like to rent a
bicycle/mountain bike
(with back-pedal
brakes).

Vorrei noleggiare una *bicicletta/mountain bike* … con il freno a contropedale. vōre'ē nōlejä're ōō'nä bētshēkle'tä/ moun'ten bīk (kōn ēl fre'nō kōntrōpedä'le).

I'd like to rent it
(for) …

La vorrei noleggiare per …
lä vōre'ē nōlejä're per …

   tomorrow.

   one day.

   two days.

   one week.

domani. dōmä'nē.

un giorno. ōōn jōr'nō.

due giorni. dōō'e jōr'nē.

una settimana. ōō'nä setēmä'nä.

73

? **Che tipo di macchina vuole?**
ke tē'pō dē mä'kēnä vōō-ō'le?

What kind of car
would you like?

How much will that
cost?

Quanto costa? kōō-än'tō kō'stä?

How much mileage is
included in the price?

**Quanti chilometri sono compresi
nel prezzo?** kōō-än'tē kēlō'metrē sō'nō
kōmpre'sē nel pre'tsō?

What kind of fuel
does it take?

Che tipo di carburante ci vuole?
ke tē'pō dē kärbōōrän'te tshē vōō-ō'le?

Is comprehensive
insurance included?

**È inclusa un'assicurazione a copertura
totale?** e ēnklōō'zä ōōnäsēkōōrätsyō'ne
ä kōpertōō'rä tōtä'le?

What's the
deductible?

**A quanto ammonta la quota a carico del
cliente?** ä kōō-än'tō ämōn'tä lä kōō-ō'tä ä
kä'rēkō del klē-en'te?

Can I return the car
in …?

**Posso riconsegnare la macchina anche
a …?** pō'sō rēkōnsenyä're lä mä'kēnä
än'ke ä …?

INFO Roads in Italy fall into various categories.
When driving on the **strada communale, the
strada provinciale** strä'dä kōmōōnä'le, strä'dä prōvēntshä'le (state
road), or the **strada statale** strä'dä stätä'le (interstate road), you
must honor the 90 km/h (app. 55 mph) speed limit. You may
drive up to 110 km/h (app. 65 mph) on the **superstrada** sōōper-
strä'dä (interstate highway) and up to 130 km/h (app. 75 mph)
on the **autostrada** outōsträ'dä (national highway).

| When do I have to be back? | **Quando devo essere di ritorno?** |
| | kōō·än'dō de'vō e'sere dē rētōr'nō? |

| I'd also like a helmet. | **Mi dia anche un casco, per favore.** |
| | mē dyä än'ke ōōn käs'kō, per fävō're. |

Parking

| Is there a *parking garage/parking lot* nearby? | **C'è un *garage/parcheggio* qui vicino?** |
| | tshe ōōn *gäräj'/pärke'jō* kōō·e' vētshē'no? |

| Is the parking lot supervised? | **Il parcheggio è custodito?** |
| | ēl pärke'jō e kōōstōdē'tō? |

| Do you pay at the exit or in advance? | **Si paga all' uscita, o devo pagare in anticipo?** sē pä'gä älōōshē'tä, ō de'vō pägä're ēn äntē'tshēpō? |

3

INFO You must pay to park in spaces marked in blue, usually by getting a receipt from a ticket machine. Parking spaces marked in white are free.

| Is the parking garage open all night? | **Il garage rimane aperto tutta la notte?** |
| | ēl gäräj' rēmä'ne äper'tō tōō'tä lä nō'te? |

| Can I park here? | **Posso parcheggiare qui?** |
| | pō'sō pärkejä're kōō·ē? |

75

Where is/How far is it to the nearest gas station?	**Dov'è/Quant'è lontano il prossimo distributore?** dōvě'/kōō-änte' lōntä'nō ēl prō'sēmō dēstrēbōōtō're?

INFO In Italy gas stations have the same opening hours as the stores. You will receive service during the working day. Many gas stations offer self-service at night or on Sundays: you must pay in advance at a machine for the amount of gas you need before filling your tank.

Fill it up, please.	**Il pieno, per favore!** ēl pye'nō, per fävō're!
… lire's worth of …, please.	**… lire di …, per favore.** … lē're dē …, per fävō're.
unleaded	**normale senza piombo** nōrmä'le sen'tsä pyōm'bō
diesel	**diesel** dē'sel
leaded	**normale** nōrmä'le
super unleaded	**super senza piombo** sōō'per sen'tsä pyōm'bō
super leaded	**super** sōō'per
two-stroke engine fuel	**miscela** mēshe'lä
Can I pay with this credit card?	**Posso pagare con questa carta di credito?** pō'sō pägä're kōn kōō·e'stä kär'tä dē kre'dētō?

I'd like *1 liter/2 liters* of oil, please.	**Vorrei *un litro/due litri* d'olio.** vōre'ē ōōn lē'trō/dōō'e lē'trē dō'lyō.
Could you change the oil, please?	**Cambi l'olio, per favore.** käm'bē lō'lyō, per fävō're.
I need snow chains.	**Mi servono delle catene da neve.** mē servō'nō de'le Käte'ne dä ne've.

INFO The **autostrada** outōsträ'dä is a toll road in Italy. You must take a card from a machine at the toll area before you can drive onto the **autostrada**. When you drive off, you must pay the amount indicated on the card for the distance (in kilometers) you have driven.

Breakdown and Accidents

3

Please call …, quickly!	**Presto, chiami …** pre'stō, kyä'mē …
an ambulance	**un'ambulanza!** ōōnämbōōlän'tsä!
the police	**la polizia!** lä pōlē'tsyä!
the fire department	**i vigili del fuoco!** ē vē'jēlē del fōō-ō-kō!
I've had an accident.	**Ho avuto un incidente.** ō ävōō'tō ōōn ēntshēden'te.
May I use your phone?	**Posso usare il Suo telefono?** pō'sō ōōzä're ēl sōō'ō tele'fōnō?
Nobody's hurt.	**Non ci sono feriti.** nōn tshē sō'nō ferē'tē.

77

... people have been (seriously) injured.	**... persone sono rimaste (gravemente) ferite.** .... persŏ'ne sŏ'nŏ rēmä'ste (grävemen'te) ferē'te.
Please help me.	**Mi aiuti, per favore!** mē äyŏō'tē, per fävŏ're!
I need a first-aid kit.	**Mi servono bende, garza e cerotti.** mē servŏ'nŏ ben'de, gär'tsä e tsherŏ'tē.
I'm out of gas.	**Non ho più benzina.** nŏn ŏ pyŏō bentsē'nä.
Could you ...	**Potrebbe ...** pŏtrē'be ...
give me a lift?	**darmi un passaggio?** där'mē ŏōn päsä'jŏ?
tow my car?	**rimorchiare la mia macchina?** rēmŏrkyä're lä mē'ä mä'kēnä?
send me a tow-truck?	**mandarmi un carro attrezzi?** mändär'mē ŏōn kä'rŏ ätre'tsē?
It's not my fault.	**Non è colpa mia.** nŏn e kŏl'pä mē'ä.
It's your fault.	**E' colpa Sua.** e kŏl'pä sŏō'ä.
You didn't have the right-of-way.	**Lei non ha rispettato la precedenza.** le'ē nŏn ä rēspetä'tŏ lä pretsheden'tsä.
I had the right of way.	**Avevo la precedenza.** äve'vŏ lä pretsheden'tsä.
You cut the corner.	**Lei ha tagliato la curva.** le'ē ä tälyä'tŏ lä kŏōr'vä.

78

You were following too closely.	**Lei non ha rispettato la distanza regolamentare.** le'ē nōn ä rēspetä'tō lä dēstän'tsä regōlämentä're.	
You were going too fast.	**Lei andava troppo forte.** le'ē ändä'vä trō'pō fōr'te.	
I was doing … kilometers an hour.	**Andavo a … chilometri all'ora.** ändä'vō ä … kēlō'metrē älō'rä.	
You damaged the …	**Ha danneggiato …** ä dänejä'tō …	
May I have your *name and address/insurance information,* please?	**Mi dia** *il Suo nome e il Suo indirizzo/il nome della Sua assicurazione,* **per favore.** mē dē'ä *ēl sōō'ō nō'me e ēl sōō'ō ēndērē'tsō/ēl nō'me de'lä sōō'ä äsēkōōrätsyō'ne,* per fävō're.	
Would you mind being a witness?	**Potrebbe testimoniare sull'accaduto?** pōtre'be testēmōnyä're sōōläkädōō'tō?	
Thank you very much for your help.	**Grazie dell'aiuto.** grä'tsē·e deläyōō'tō.	

3

> **!**
> • **I Suoi documenti, per favore.** ē sōō·oi' dōkōōmen'tē, per fävō're.

Your driver's license, registration, and insurance information, please.

> **!**
> • *La Sua patente/Il Suo libretto de circolazione,* **per favore!** lä sōō'a päten'te/ēl sōō'ō lēbre'tō de tshērkōlätsēō'ne, per fävō're!

Your *driver's licence/registration,* please.

79

Do it yourself

Could you lend me ..., please?

Per favore, mi potrebbe prestare …?
per fävō're, mē pōtre'be prestä're …?

I need …

Mi servirebbe … mē servēre'be …

a bicycle repair kit.

il corredo per la riparazione di forature. ēl kōre'do per lä rēpärätsyō'ne dē fōrätōō're.

a pump.

una pompa dell'aria.
ōō'nä pōm'pä delär'yä.

a (…) wrench.

una chiave inglese (da …).
ōō'nä kyä've ēn·gle'se (dä …).

a screwdriver.

un cacciavite. ōōn kätshävē'te.

a (…) socket wrench.

una chiave fissa a tubo (da …).
ōō'nä kyä've fē'sä ä tōō'bō (dä …).

a jack.

un cric. ōōn krēk.

a tool kit.

una scatola degli attrezzi.
ōō'nä skä'tōlä de'lyē ätre'tsē.

a pair of pliers.

una tenaglia. ōō'nä tenä'lyä.

At the Repair Shop

Where is the nearest (...) garage?	**Dov'è l'officina (concessionaria) più vicina?** dōve' lōfētshē'nä (kōntshesyōnär'yä) pyōō vētshē'nä?
My car's on the road to ...	**La mia macchina sta sulla strada per ...** lä mē'ä mä'kēnä stä (sōō'lä strä'dä per) ...
Can you tow it away?	**La potete rimorchiare?** lä pōte'te rēmōrkyä're?
Would you have a look at it?	**Può dare un'occhiata?** pōō-ō' dä're ōōnōkyä'tä?
... is broken.	**... non funziona.** ... non fōōntsyō'nä.
My car won't start.	**La mia macchina non parte.** lä mē'ä mä'kēnä nōn pär'te.
The battery is dead.	**La batteria è scarica.** lä bäterē'ä e skä'rēkä.
The engine *sounds funny/doesn't have any power.*	**Il motore *fa dei rumori strani/non tira.*** ēl mōtō're fä de'ē rōōmō'rē strä'nē/nōn tē'rä.
Do you have the (original) parts for ... ?	**Ha pezzi di ricambio (originali) per ... ?** ä pe'tsē dē rēkäm'byō (ōrējēnä'lē) per ...?

3

Just do the essential repairs, please.	**Faccia soltanto le riparazioni più necessarie, per favore.** fä'shä sōltän'tō le rēpärätsyō'nē pyōō netshesär'ye, per fävō're.
When will it be ready?	**Per quando sarà pronta?** per kōō·än'dō särä' prōn'tä?
Can I still drive it?	**Posso ancora andarci in giro?** pō'sō änkō'rä ändär'tshē ēn jē'rō?

Car, Motorbike and Bike

to accelerate	**accelerare** ätshelerä're
accident	**l'incidente** *m* lēntshēden'te
air filter	**il filtro dell'aria** ēl fēl'trō delär'yä
antifreeze	**l'antigelo** läntje'lō
automatic transmission	**il cambio automatico** ēl käm'byō outomä'tēko
battery	**la batteria** lä bäterē'ä
bicycle	**la bicicletta** lä bētshēkle'tä
brake	**il freno** ēl fre'nō
– fluid	**l'olio dei freni** lō'lyō de'ē fre'nē
– lights	**le luci d'arresto** le lōō'tshē däre'stō
bright lights	**il faro abbagliante** ēl fä'rō äbälyän'te
broken	**rotto** rō'tō
bulb	**la lampadina** lä lämpädē'nä
bumper	**il paraurti** ēl pärä·ōōr'tē
car	**la macchina** lä mä'kēnä
carburetor	**il carburatore** ēl kärbōōrätō're

catalytic converter	**la marmitta catalitica**
	lä märmë´tä kätälë´tëkä
to change	**cambiare** kämbyä´re
child seat	**il seggiolino per l'auto**
	ël sejölë´nö per lou´tö
clutch	**la frizione** lä frëtsyö´ne
state road	**la strada provinciale**
	lä strä´dä provëntshä´le
curve	**la curva** lä kōōr´vä
to drive	**andare (in macchina)**
	ändä´re (ën mä´kënä)
driver's license	**la patente** lä päten´te
dynamo	**la dinamo** lä dë´nämö
emergency brake	**il freno a mano** ël fre´nö ä mä´nö
engine	**il motore** ël mötö´re
exhaust	**lo scappamento** lö skäpämen´tö
fan belt	**la cinghia**
	lä tshën´gë·ä
fender	**il parafango** ël päräfän´gö
first-aid kit	**la cassetta di pronto soccorso**
	lä käse´tä dë pron´tö sökör´sö
four-wheel drive car	**il fuoristrada** ël fōō-örësträ´dä
fuse	**il fusibile** ël fōōzë´bële
garage	**l'officina** löfëtshe´nä
gas *(liquid fuel)*	**la benzina** lä bentse´nä
gas *(gaseous fuel)*	**il gas** ël gäs
– station	**il distributore** ël dëstrëbōōtö´re
gear	**la marcia** lä mär´tshä
headlights	**il faro** ël fä´rö

3

helmet	**il casco** ēl käs′kō
highway	**l'autostrada** loutōsträ′dä
horn	**il clacson** ēl kläk′sōn
ignition	**l'accensione** f lätshensyō′ne
injured	**ferito** ferē′tō
innertube	**la camera d'aria** lä kä′merä där′yä
insurance	**l'assicurazione** f läsēkōōrätsyō′ne
international car insurance verification	**il carnet di assistenza internazionale** ēl kärne′ dē äsēsten′tsä ēnternätsyōnä′le
interstate road	**la (strada) statale** lä (strä′dä) stätä′le
joint	**la guarnizione** lä gōō-ärnētsyō′ne
kilometer	**il chilometro** ēl kēlō′metrō
light	**la luce** lä lōō′tshe
low beams	**il faro anabbagliante** ēl fä′rō änäbälyän′te
mirror	**lo specchio** lō spe′kyō
motorcycle	**la motocicletta** lä mōtōtshēkle′tä
neutral	**la marcia in folle** lä mär′tshä ēn fō′le
no parking	**il divieto di parcheggio** ēl dēvye′tō dē pärke′jō
oil	**l'olio del motore** lō′lyō del mōtō′re
– change	**il cambio dell'olio** ēl käm′byō delō′lyō
to park	**parcheggiare** pärkejä′re
parking garage	**il garage** ēl gäräj′
parking light	**le luci di posizione** le lōō′tshe dē pōzētsyō′ne
parking lot	**il parcheggio** ēl pärke′jō

84

parking meter	**il parchimetro** ēl pärkē'metrō	
parking receipt machine	**il distributore automatico di biglietti per il parcheggio** ēl dēstrēbōōtō're outōmä'tēkō dē bēlye'tē per ēl pärke'jō	
to put into gear	**innestare la marcia** ēnestä're lä mär'tshä	
radiator	**il radiatore** ēl rädyätō're	
rear-end collision	**il tamponamento** ēl tämpōnämen'tō	
registration number	**il numero di targa** ēl nōō'merō dē tär'gä	
to rent	**noleggiare** nōlejä're	
to repair	**riparare** rēpärä're	
seatbelt	**la cintura di sicurezza** lä tshintōō'rä dē sēkōōre'tsä	
shock absorber	**l'ammortizzatore** *m* lämōrtētsätō're	**3**
snow chains	**le catene da neve** le käte'ne dä ne've	
spare gas canister	**la tanica di riserva** lä tä'nēkä dē rēzer'vä	
spare part	**il pezzo di ricambio** ēl pe'tsō dē rēkäm'byō	
spare tire	**la ruota di scorta** lä rōō-ō'tä dē skōr'tä	
spark plug	**la candela d'accensione** lä kände'lä dätshensyō'ne	
starter	**lo starter** lō stär'ter	
steering	**lo sterzo** lō ster'tsō	
tail light	**il fanalino posteriore** ēl fänälē'nō pōsteryō're	
tire	**la ruota** lä rōō-ō'tä	

toll	**il pedaggio** ēl pedä'jō
– booth	**il casello autostradale**
	ēl käse'lō outōsträdä'le
– road	**il tratto stradale soggetto a pedaggio**
	ēl trä'tō strädä'le sōje'tō ä pedä'jō
to tow (away)	**rimorchiare** rēmōrkyä're
tow rope	**il cavo da rimorchio**
	ēl kä'vō dä rēmōr'kyō
tow truck	**il carro attrezzi** ēl kä'rō ätre'tsē
transmission	**il cambio** ēl käm'byō
turn indicator	**la freccia** lä fre'tshä
unleaded	**senza piombo** sen'tsä pyōm'bō
valve	**la valvola** lä väl'vōlä
vehicle registration	**il libretto di circolazione**
	ēl lēbre'tō dē tshērkōlätsyō'ne
warning sign	**il triangolo** ēl trē·an'gōlō
water	**l'acqua** lä'kōō·ä
distilled -	**l'acqua distillata** lä'kōō·ä dēstēlä'tä
wheel	**la ruota** lä rōō·ō'tä
windshield wiper	**le spazzole del tergicristallo**
blades	le spä'tsōle del terjēkrēstä'lō

BUS, SUBWAY, TAXI

By Bus and Subway

Where's the nearest subway station?	**Dov'è la fermata della metropolitana più vicina?** dōve' lä fermä'tä de'lä metrōpōlētä'nä pyōō vētshe'nä?

INFO In Italy only Rome, Milan, and Naples have a subway system. The entrance to the subway is indicated by a sign with a white **"M"** e'me across a green background. **"M"** stands for **metropolitana**, or **metro** me'trō for short. In Venice there is of course no bus system. You can take a gondola – or a **vaporetto** väpōre'tō (motor boat), as the Venetians do.

Where's the *bus/streetcar* stop for ...?	**Dove ferma *l'autobus/il tram* per ...?** dō've fer'mä *lou'tōbōōs/ēl träm* per ...?
Which *bus/streetcar* goes to ...?	**Quale *autobus/tram* va a ...?** kōō·ä'le *ou'tōbōōs/träm* vä ä ...?
! Il numero ... ēl nōō'merō ...	Number ...
! La linea ... lä lē'ne·ä	The ... line.
When is the next *bus/streetcar* to ...?	**Quando parte il prossimo *autobus/tram* per ...?** kōō·än'dō pär'te ēl prō'semō *ou'tōbōōs/träm* per ...?

87

When does the last *bus/streetcar* return?	**Quando riparte l'ultimo *autobus/tram*?** kōō·än'dō rēpär'te lōōl'tēmō *ou'tōbōōs/träm*?
Does the bus have the same schedule on *Saturdays/Sundays*?	**Di *sabato/domenica* l'autobus viaggia agli stessi orari?** dē sä'bätō/dōme'nēkä lou'tōbōōs vyä'jä ä'lye ste'sē örä'rē?

INFO Cross-country buses are often quicker and cheaper than trains. Ask about them at the local tourist bureau, since the bus companies differ from region to region. The color of the buses has nothing to do with the routes. There are bus stations in larger towns; in smaller towns, there are always special stops. One can often purchase tickets in the bus itself.

Does this *bus/ streetcar* go to ...?	*Quest'autobus/Questo* **tram va a ... ?** kōō·estou'tōbōōs/kōō·e'sto träm vä ä ...?
Do I have to transfer to get to ...?	**Per andare a ... devo cambiare?** per ändä're ä ... de'vō kämbyä're?
Could you tell me where I have to *get off/transfer*, please?	**Per favore, mi dice dove devo *scendere/ cambiare?*** per fävō're, mē dē'tshe dō've de'vō shen'dere/kämbyä're?
Where can I get a ticket?	**Dove si comprano i biglietti?** dō've sē kömprä'nō ē bēlye'tē?
I'd like a ticket to ..., please.	**Un biglietto per ..., per favore.** ōōn bēlye'tō per ..., per fävō're.

INFO You can usually buy bus tickets in the **bar** bär, at the tobacconist's, and at newsstands. It's a good idea to get the **biglietti multipli** bēlyeʹtē mōōlʹtēplē (tickets valid for several trips), since they end up being cheaper than single tickets.

Are there ...	**Ci sono ...** tshē sōʹnō ...
tickets valid for several trips?	**biglietti multipli?** bēlyeʹtē mōōlʹtēplē?
day passes?	**biglietti giornalieri?** bēlyeʹtē jörnälyeʹrē
weekly tickets?	**abbonamenti settimanali?** äbōnämenʹtē setēmänäʹlē?

Taxi!

3

Where can I get a taxi?	**Dov'è un posteggio di taxi?** dōveʹ ōōn pōsteʹjō dē täʹksē?
Could you order a taxi for me for ... o'clock?	**Mi potrebbe chiamare un taxi per le ...?** mē pōtreʹbe kyämäʹre ōōn täʹksē per le ...?
Could you take me ..., please?	**..., per favore.** ..., per fävōʹre.
to the train station	**Alla stazione** äʹlä stätsyōʹne
to the airport	**All'aeroporto** älä-erōpōrʹtō
to the ... Hotel	**All'hotel ...** älōtelʹ ...
to the center of town	**In centro** ēn tshenʹtrō
to ...	**A ...** ä ...

89

INFO To avoid nasty surprises, always make sure to take only official taxis. These will always be standing at designated taxi stands and have the appropriate taxi sign on the roof of the car.

How much is it to …?	**Quanto costa per andare a … ?** kōō·än'tō kō'stä per ändä're ä …?
No, thanks, that's too expensive for me.	**No, grazie, per me è troppo caro.** nō, grä'tsē·e, per me e trö'pō kä'rō.
Is there an extra charge for baggage?	**Si paga una tariffa extra per i bagagli?** sē pä'gä ōō'nä tärē'fä ek'strä per ē bägä'lyē?
Would you *start/reset* the taxometer, please?	*Accenda/Azzeri* **il tassametro, per favore!** ätshen'dä/ädze're ēl täsä'metrō, per fävō're.
Could you *wait/stop* here (for a moment), please?	*Aspetti/Si fermi* **(un attimo) qui, per favore!** äspe'tē/sē fer'mē (ōōn ä'tēmō) kōō·ē', per fävō're.

Bus, Subway, Taxi

bus	**l'autobus** *m* lou'tōbōōs
cross-country –	**il pullman** ēl pōōl'män
– station	**la stazione dei pullman** lä stätsyō'ne dē pōōlmän
city center	**il centro** ēl tshen'tro
day pass	**il biglietto giornaliero** ēl bēlye'tō jōrnälye'rō

departure	**la partenza** lä pärten'tsä
direction	**la direzione** lä dēretsyō'ne
driver	**l'autista** *m* loutē'stä
to get out	**scendere** shen'dere
last stop	**il capolinea** ēl käpōlē'ne·ä
receipt	**la ricevuta** lä rētshevōō'tä
schedule	**l'orario** lōrär'yō
to stamp *(a ticket)*	**timbrare** tēmbrä're
stop	**la fermata** lä fermä'tä
to stop	**fermare** fermä're
streetcar	**il tram** ēl träm
subway	**la metropolitana** lä metrōpōlētä'nä
taxi	**il taxi** ēl tä'ksē
– stand	**il posteggio di taxi** ēl pōste'jō dē tä'ksē
ticket	**il biglietto** ēl bēlye'tō
– (vending) machine	**il distributore automatico di biglietti** ēl dēstrēbōōtō're outōmä'tēkō dē bēlye'tē
– stamping machine	**la macchina obliteratrice** lä mä'kēnä ōblēterätrē'tshe
to transfer	**cambiare** kämbyä're
weekly ticket	**l'abbonamento settimanale** läbōnämen'tō setēmänä'le

3

HITCHHIKING

I'd like to go to ...	**Vorrei andare a ...** vōre'ē ändä're ä ...
Where/Which way are you going?	**Lei dove va?** le'ē dō've vä?
Can you take me (part of the way) there?	**Mi può dare un passaggio (per un tratto)?** mē pōō-ō' dä're ōōn päsä'jō (per ōōn trä'tō)?

? **Dove vuole scendere?**
dō've vōō-ō'le shen'dere?
Where do you want to get out?

| Could you let me out here, please? | **Mi faccia scendere qui, per favore.** mē fä'tshä shen'dere kōō-ē', per fävō're. |
| Thanks for the lift. | **Grazie mille per il passaggio.** grä'tsē-e mē'le per ēl päsä'jō. |

Food and Drink

MENÙ MENU

Antipasti Appetizers

acciughe *f/pl* ätshōō'ge	anchovies
affettato *m* **(misto)** äfetä'tō (mē'stō)	cold cut platter
carciofini *m/pl* **sott'olio** kärtshōfē'nē sōtō'lyō	artichoke hearts in oil
carpaccio *m* kärpä'tshō	thinly-sliced raw beef tenderized with lemon juice and oil
crostini *m/pl* **misti** krōstē'nē mē'stē	toasted bread with various toppings
funghi *m/pl* **sott'olio** fōōn'gē sōtō'lyō	mushrooms in oil
gamberi *m/pl* gämbe'rē	crawfish
ostriche *f/pl* ō'strēke	oysters
prosciutto *m* prōshōō'tō	ham
– cotto – kō'tō	cooked –
– crudo – krōō'dō	cured –
– con fichi freschi – kōn fē'kē fres'kē	– with fresh figs
– e melone – e melō'ne	– with melon
salame *m* sälä'me	salami
sottaceti *m/pl* sōtätshe'tē	pickled vegetables
tartine *f/pl* tärtē'ne	canapés

Primi piatti   First Courses

Minestre   Soups

brodo *m* brō'dō
broth

minestra *f* mēnes'trä
soup

  – di verdura – dē verdōō'rä
    vegetable soup

minestrone *m* mēnestrō'ne
thick vegetable soup

pastina *f* **in brodo**
pästē'nä ēn brō'dō
broth with small pasta

zuppa *f* **di pesce**
tsōō'pä dē pe'she
fish soup

Pasta e riso   Pasta and Rice

agnolotti *m/pl* änyōlō'tē
stuffed pasta

cannelloni *m/pl* känelō'nē
filled rolls of pasta

fettuccine *f/pl* fetōōtshē'ne
flat pasta

fusilli *m/pl* fōōzē'lē
spiral pasta

gnocchi *m/pl* nyō'kē
small potato
dumplings

lasagne *f/pl* läzä'nye
lasagne

pasta *f* **(asciutta)**
pä'stä äshōō'tä
pasta dish

  – al burro (in bianco)
  – äl bōō'rō (ēn byän'kō)
    – with butter or olive oil
    and cheese

  – al pomodoro
  – äl pōmōdō'rō
    – with tomato sauce

  – al ragù – äl rägōō'
    – with meat sauce

  – alla carbonara
  – ä'lä kärbōnä'rä
    – with bacon and egg

4

– alla panna – ä'lä pä'nä	– with cream sauce
– al pesto – äl pe'stō	– with pesto sauce
– alle vongole	– with clams
– ä'le vōn'gōle	
penne *f/pl* pe'ne	short, straight macaroni
polenta *f* pōlen'tä	cornmeal porridge
tagliatelle *f/pl* tälyäte'le	flat pasta
vermicelli *m/pl* vermētshe'lē	thin pasta
risotto *m* rēsō'tō	rice dish
– ai funghi (porcini)	– with mushrooms
– ī fōōn'gē (pōrtshē'nē)	
– alla marinara	– with seafood
– ä'lä märänä'rä	

Carni *Meat*

agnello *m* änye'lō	lamb
coniglio *m* kōnē'lyō	rabbit
maiale *m* mäyä'le	pork
maialino *m* **da latte**	suckling pig
mäyälē'nō dä lä'te	
manzo *m* män'tsō	beef
montone *m* mōntō'ne	mutton
vitello *m* vēte'lō	veal
arrosto *m* ärō'stō	roast
bistecca *f* bēste'kä	steak
braciola *f* brätshō'lä	chop
brasato *m* bräzä'tō	beef braised in wine
coscia *m* **di vitello**	leg of veal
kō'shä dē vēte'lō	

costoletta *f* kōstōle'tä	cutlet
cotoletta *f* **alla milanese**	breaded veal cutlet
kōstōle'tä ä'lä mēläne'ze	
fegato *m* fe'gätō	liver
fesa *f* **di vitello** fe'zä dē vēte'lo	veal cutlet
fettina *f* fetēnä	thinly-sliced cutlet
filetto *m* fēle'tō	filet
frattaglie *f/pl* frätä'lyē	organ meats
involtini *m/pl* ēnvōlte'nē	roulades
lombata *f* lōmbä'tä	loin
ossobuco *m* ōsōbōō'kō	knuckle of beef or veal cut horizontally in slices
petto *m* **di vitello**	breast of veal
pe'tō dē vēte'lo	
polpette *f/pl* pōlpe'te	meatballs
ragù *m* rägōō'	ragout
salsicce *f/pl* sälsē'tshe	sausages
scaloppine *f/pl* skälōpe'nē	small cutlet
spezzatino *m* spetsäte'nō	stew
spiedini *m/pl* **alla griglia**	shish kebab
spyede'nē ä'lä grē'lyä	
stufato *m* stōōfä'tō	stew
vitello *m* **tonnato**	veal with tuna and
vēte'lō tōnä'tō	caper sauce

4

Pollame *Poultry*

anitra *f* **all'arancia**　　　duck à l'orange
ä'nēträ älärän'shä
fagiano *m*　fäjä'nō　　　　pheasant
faraona *f*　färä·ō'nä　　　guinea fowl
gallina *f*　gälē'nä　　　　hen
oca *f*　ō'kä　　　　　　　goose
petto *m* **di pollo**　pe'tō dē pō'lō　chicken breast
pollo *m*　pō'lō　　　　　chicken
　– arrosto – ärō'stō　　　roast chicken
tacchino *m*　täkē'nō　　　turkey

Pesce *Fish*

anguilla *f*　än·gōō·ē'lä　　eel
aringa *f*　ärēn'gä　　　　herring
calamari *m/pl*　kälämä'rē　squid fried in rings
carpa *f*　kär'pä　　　　　carp
frittura *f* **di pesce**　　　mixed fried fish
frētōō'rä dē pe'she
luccio *m*　lōō'tshō　　　　pike
pesce *m* **spada**　pe'she spä'dä　swordfish
rombo *m*　rōm'bō　　　　turbot
salmone *m*　sälmō'ne　　　salmon
sogliola *f*　sōlyō'lä　　　　sole
storione *m*　stōryō'ne　　　sturgeon
tonno *m*　tō'nō　　　　　tuna
triglia *f*　trē'lyä　　　　　red mullet
trota trō'tä　　　　　　　trout

98

Crostacei e molluschi — *Seafood*

aragosta *f* ärägö'stä	lobster
cozze *f/pl* kö'tse	mussels
frutti *m/pl* **di mare**	seafood
frōō'tē dē mä're	
gamberetti *m/pl* gämbere'tē	shrimps
gambero *m* gäm'berō	crawfish
ostriche *f/pl* ö'strëke	oysters
polpo *m* pöl'pō	octopus
vongole *f/pl* vōn'gōle	clams

Verdura e contorni — *Vegetables and Side Dishes*

asparagi *m/pl* äspä'räjē	asparagus
bietole *f/pl* byetö'le	Swiss chard
carciofi *m/pl* kärtshö'fē	artichokes
– fritti – frē'tē	fried –
cavolfiore *m* kävölfyō're	cauliflower
ceci *m/pl* tshe'tshē	chickpeas
fagioli *m/pl* fäjō'lē	beans
– bianchi di Spagna	broad –
byän'kē dē spä'nyä	
fagiolini *m/pl* fäjōlē'nē	green –
finocchi *m/pl* fēnö'kē	fennel
funghi *m/pl* fōōn'gē	mushrooms
– coltivati – költēvä'tē	cultivated –
– porcini – pörtshē'nē	porcini –
indivia *f* ēndē'vyä	endive
melanzane *f/pl* meläntsä'ne	eggplants

99

patate *f/pl* pätä'te
  – arrosto – ärō'stō
  – fritte – frē'te
  – lesse – le'se
  peperonata *f* peperōnä'tä

peperoni *m/pl* peperō'nē
piselli *m/pl* pise'lē
pomodori *m/pl* pōmōdō'rē
spinaci *m/pl* spēnä'tshe
zucchine *f/pl* tsōōkē'ne
  – ripiene – rēpye'ne

potatoes
  – baked potato
  French fries
  boiled potatoes
thinly sliced peppers cooked
with onions and tomatoes

peppers
peas
tomatoes
spinach
zucchini
  – stuffed – au gratin

Insalate *Salads*

insalata *f* ēnsälä'tä
  – di cetrioli – dē tshetrē·ō'lē
  – mista – mē'stä
  – di pomodori
  – dē pōmōdō'rē
tonno *m* **e fagioli**
tō'nō e fäjō'lē

salad
  cucumber salad
  mixed salad
  tomato salad

salad of broad beans and tuna
with onions

Uova *Egg Dishes*

frittata *f* frētä'tä
tortino *m* **di carciofi**
törtē'nō dē kärtshō'fē

omelette
pancake with artichoke hearts

Modi di preparazione	Methods of Preparation
affumicato äfōōmēkä'tō	smoked
a vapore ä väpō're	steamed
ai ferri ī fe'rē	broiled
al cartoccio äl kärtō'tshō	baked in foil
al forno äl fōr'nō	baked
alla brace ä'lä brä'tshe	grilled on a brazier
alla griglia ä'lä grē'lyä	grilled on a barbecue
allo spiedo ä'lō spye'dō	on a skewer
arrosto ärō'stō	roasted
farcito färtshē'tō	stuffed
fatto in casa fä'tō ēn kä'sä	homemade
fritto frē'tō	deep-fried
gratinato grätēnä'tō	au gratin
ripieno rēpye'nō	filled
stufato stōōfä'tō	steamed

Formaggi	Cheese
Bel paese *m* bel pä-e'ze	soft, mild cheese
formaggio *m* **grattugiato** fōrmä'jō grätōōjä'tō	grated cheese
gorgonzola *m* gōrgōndzō'lä	blue cheese
mozzarella *f* **di bufala** mōtsäre'lä dē bōō'fälä	buffalo mozzarella
parmigiano *m* pärmējä'nō	Parmesan cheese
pecorino *m* pekōrē'nō	sheep's cheese
stracchino *m* sträke'nō	soft, mild cheese

4

Dolci   Desserts

➡ see also Bar, Gelateria, Pasticceria (p. 104)

budino *m* bōōdē'nō	pudding
cassata *f* käsä'tä	ice cream with candied fruits
crema *f* kre'mä	custard
crème *f* **caramel** krem kärämel'	crème caramel
macedonia *f* mätshedō'nyä	fruit salad
mousse *f* **al cioccolato** mōōs äl tshōkōlä'tō	chocolate mousse
zabaione *m* dzäbäyō'ne	cream made of egg yolks, sugar and Marsala
zuppa *f* **inglese** tsōō'pä ēn·gle'se	trifle

Frutta   Fruit

anguria *f* ängōōr'yä	watermelon
arancia *f* ärän'tshä	orange
ciliege *f*/*pl* tshēlye'je	cherries
fico *m* 'fē'kō	fig
fragole *f*/*pl* frä'gōle	strawberries
lamponi *m*/*pl* lämpō'nē	raspberries
mela *f* me'lä	apple
melone *m* melō'ne	melon
pera *f* pe'rä	pear
pesca *f* pe'skä	peach
uva *f* ōō'vä	grape

BEVANDE   BEVERAGES

Vini   *Wine and Champagne*

vino *m* ve'nō	wine
– bianco– byän'kō	white –
– rosso– rō'sō	red –
– rosé– rōze'	rosé –
– da tavola– dä tä'vōlä	table –
– della casa– de'lä kä'sä	house –
– in bottiglia– ēn bōtē'lyä	– by the bottle
prosecco *m* prōse'kō	sparkling wine from the Veneto region
spumante *m* spōōmän'te	sparkling wine
dolce dōl'tsche	sweet
demi-sec demē-sek'	medium-dry
secco se'kō	dry

Altre bevande alcoliche   *Other Alcoholic Drinks*

birra *f* bē'rä	beer
– alla spina – ä'lä spē'nä	draft –
– chiara – kyä'rä	blond –
– scura – skōō'rä	dark –
amaretto *m* ämäre'tō	amaretto
amaro *m* ämä'rō	bitters
grappa *f* grä'pä	strong brandy
liquore *m* lēkōō-ō're	liqueur
marsala *m* märsä'lä	Marsala wine
sambuca *f* sämbōō'kä	anis liqueur
stravecchio *m* strävek'yō	well-aged cognac

4

Bevande analcoliche	Non-alcoholic Drinks
acqua *f* **minerale** ä'kōō-ä mēnerä'le	mineral water
– gassata – gäsä'tä	carbonated –
– naturale – nätōōrä'le	non-carbonated –
aranciata *f* äräntshä'tä	orange soda
frappé *m* fräpe'	milkshake
limonata *f* lēmōnä'tä	lemon soda
spremuta *f* **di arancia** spremōō'tä dē ärän'tshä	freshly-squeezed orange juice
spremuta *f* **di limone** spremōō'tä dē lēmō'ne	freshly-squeezed lemon juice
succo *m* **di frutta** sōō'kō dē frōō'tä	fruit juice
– d'arancia – därän'tshä	orange juice
– di mele – dē me'le	apple juice

BAR CAFÉ

caffè *m* **(espresso)** käfe' (espre'sō)	espresso
– corretto – kōre'tō	– with liqueur
– lungo – lōōn'gō	– diluted with a bit of water
– macchiato – mäkyä'tō	– with milk
– ristretto – rēstre'tō	very strong –

cappuccino *m* käpŏŏtshē'nŏ — cappuccino

camomilla *f* kämŏmē'lä — camomile tea

cioccolata *f* tshŏkŏlä'tä — hot chocolate

latte *m* lä'te — milk

  – macchiato mäkyä'tŏ — – with coffee

tè *m* te — hot tea

  – al latte – äl lä'te — – with milk

  – al limone – äl lēmŏ'ne — – with lemon

GELATERIA ICE CREAM

gelato *m* jelä'tŏ — ice cream

  – affogato – äfŏgä'tŏ — – topped with liqueur or coffee

  – alla frutta – ä'lä frŏŏ'tä — fruit –

  – alla crema – ä'lä kre'mä — rich –

  – con la panna — – with whipped cream

  – kŏn lä pä'nä

  – fior di latte – fyŏr dē lä'te — – made with cream

ghiacciolo *m* gyätshŏ'lŏ — popsicle

granita *f* gränē'tä — grainy kind of sherbet

semifreddo *m* semēfre'dŏ — semi-frozen ice cream or cake

tartufo *m* tärtŏŏ·fŏ — chocolate-covered ice cream

4

PASTICCERIA CAKES

amaretti *m/pl* ämäre'tē — almond cookies

bignè *m* bēnye' — cream puffs

bombolone *m* bōmbōlō'ne — filled donuts

brioche *f* brē-ōsh' — croissants

ciambella *f* tshämbe'lä — fried yeast pastry

crostata *f* krōstä'tä — tart

diplomatico *m* dēplōmä'tēkō — pastry with cream and liqueur

meringa *f* merēn'gä — meringue

pan *m* **di Spagna** pän dē spä'nyä — pound cake

panna *f* **montata** pä'nä mōntä'tä — whipped cream

pasticcini *m/pl* pästētshē'nē — tea cakes

sfogliatella *f* sfōlyäte'lä — pastry filled with jam or cream

torta *f* tōr'tä — cake

– **al cioccolato** – äl tshōkōlä'tō — – chocolate

– **alla frutta** – ä'lä frōō'tä — – with fruit

– **di mandorle** – dē män'dōrle — almond –

– **di mele** – dē me'le — – with apples

– **gelato** – jelä'tō — ice cream –

INFORMATION

Is there a … around here?	**Scusi, c'è … qui vicino?** skōō'zē, tshe … kōō-ē' vētshē'nō?
a good restaurant	**un buon ristorante** ōōn bōō-ōn' rēstōrän'te
an inexpensive restaurant	**un ristorante non troppo caro** ōōn rēstōrän'te nōn trō'pō kä'rō
a restaurant typical of the area	**un ristorante tipico** ōōn rēstōrän'te tē'pēkō
a bar	**un bar** ōōn bär
a café	**un caffè** ōōn käfe'

INFO You won't get a pizza in a **ristorante** rēstōrän'te; here, you usually order a four-course meal: **antipasto** äntēpä'stō (appetizer), **primo** prē'mō (soup or a pasta or a rice dish), **secondo** sekōn'dō (meat or fish), and **dolce** dōl'tshe (dessert). If you don't wish to eat all four courses, you can order a **secondo** or a **primo**. If you wish to have a side dish of anything with your **secondo** (which will consist of the meat or fish dish and nothing else) you must order it as well. **Coperto** kōper'tō is the cover charge for cutlery, tablecloth, and bread.

4

Could you reserve me a table for … people for … o'clock?	**Mi potrebbe riservare un tavolo per … persone per le …?** mē pōtre'be rēzervä're ōōn tä'vōlō per … per sō'ne per le …?

107

INFO A **trattoria** trätörĕ'ä is a more informal, inexpensive restaurant that offers dishes that are typical of the area. Recently, more expensive restaurants have begun to call themselves **trattorie** in order to suggest a rustic ambience.

A **pizzeria** pētserĕ'ä might only be open in the evenings since Italians don't eat **pizza** during the day. They also offer other dishes in addition to **pizza**. You can order just a **primo** prē'mōor **dolce** dōl'tshe in the **pizzeria**, something particularly popular with young people after the movies or the theater. If you feel like eating **pizza** during the day, you'll have to find a **pizzeria** that serves **pizza al taglio** pē'tsä äl tä'lyō(pizza slices), which you can eat there standing or take out.

A table for ..., please.	**Un tavolo per ... persone, per favore.** ōōn tä'vōlō per ... persō'ne, per fävō're.
May I have this *table/seat*?	**È libero questo *tavolo/posto*?** e lē'berō kōō·e'stō *tä'vōlō/pō'stō*?
Do you have a highchair?	**Avete un seggiolone?** äve'te ōōn sejōlō'ne?
Excuse me, where are the rest rooms?	**Scusi, dov'è la toilette?** skōō'zē, dōve' lä tōō·älet'?

❗ **Qui a *destra/sinistra*.** ● kōō·ē·'ä *des'trä/sēnēs'trä*.	Down there on the *right/left*.

108

WAITER!

May I see the menu, please?

Il menù, per favore.
ēl menōō', per fävō're.

INFO
To call the waiter, say **"Cameriere!"** kämerye're!
To call the waitress, **"Cameriera!"** kämerye'rä!

I'd like to eat something.

Vorrei mangiare qualcosa.
vōre'ē mänjä're kōō-älkō'sä.

I'd just like something small to eat.

Vorrei fare soltanto uno spuntino.
vōre'ē fä're sōltän'tō ōō'nō spōōntē'nō.

I just want something to drink.

Vorrei soltanto bere qualcosa.
vōre'ē sōltän'tō be're kōō-älkō'sä.

Unfortunately we don't have much time.

Purtroppo non abbiamo molto tempo.
pōōrtrō'pō nōn äbyä'mō mōl'tō tem'pō.

INFO During the day, you might want to try out the **tavola calda** tä'vōlä käl'dä, a kind of cafeteria where you can get inexpensive hot food at a counter. The **rosticceria** rōstētsherē'ä is also an informal type of restaurant, open only during the day. There you may get various foods such as roast chicken and vegetables or lasagne, which you can take out or sometimes eat there.

The **paninoteca** pänēnōte'kä is a relatively new kind of fast-food restaurant. You can get hot and cold **panini** pänē'nē (sandwiches) there.

4

109

? **Che cosa desidera da bere?**
kē kō'sä desē'derä dä be're?

What would you like
to drink?

I'd like ..., please. **Vorrei ...** vōre'ē ...

a glass of red wine	**un bicchiere di vino rosso.** ōōn bēkye're dē vē'nō rō'sō.
a bottle of beer	**una bottiglia di birra.** ōō'nä bōtē'lyä dē bē'rä.
a liter/half a liter of white wine	**un/mezzo litro di vino bianco.** ōōn/me'tsō lē'trō di vē'nō byän'kō.
a quarter of a liter of rosé	**un quarto di vino rosé.** ōōn kōō·är'tō dē vē'nō rōze'.
a caraffe of water	**una caraffa d'acqua.** ōō'nä kärä'fä dä'kōō·ä.
a cup of coffee	**una tazza di caffè.** ōō'nä tä'tsä dē käfe'.

Do you also have
wine by the glass?

Ha anche del vino sfuso?
ä än'ke del vē'nō sfu'zō?

INFO You can order a single glass of wine only at a
bar bär. In restaurants and pizzerias you must
order wine by the 1/4, 1/2, or full liter. A **bar** is not like an
American bar; you go there for coffees and other hot and cold
beverages as well as aperitifs. If you order a **caffè** käfe', you will
get an **espresso** espre'sō; **cappuccino** käpōōtshē'no is **espresso**
with frothed milk. In private homes you often get **caffèlatte**
käfelä'te, coffee with warm but unfrothed milk.

? **Che cosa desidera (mangiare)?** What would you like
ke kō'sä desē'derä (mänjä're)? to eat?

I would like a serving **Vorrei una porzione di …**
of … vōre'ē ōō'nä pōrtsyō'ne dē …

I'd like a piece of … **Vorrei un pezzo di …**
vōre'ē ōōn pe'tsō dē …

Do you have … ? **Ha …?** ä …?

What would you **Che cosa mi consiglia?**
recommend? ke kō'sä mē kōnsē'lyä?

! **Le consiglio …** le kōnse'lyō … I can recommend …

Do you have any **Quali sono le specialità della regione?**
regional specialties? kōō·ä'lē sō'nō le spetshälētä' de'lä
rejō'ne?

Do you serve … **Avete …** äve'te …

diabetic meals? **cibi per diabetici?**
tshē'bē per dyäbe'tētshē?

special diet **cibi dietetici?** tshē'bē dyete'tētshē?
meals?
vegetarian dishes? **piatti vegetariani?**
pyä'tē vejetäryä'nē?

Can we get a **È possibile avere una mezza porzione**
children's portion? **per i bambini?** e pōse'bēle äve're ōō'nä
me'tsä pōrtsyō'ne per ē bämbē'nē?

4

Does it have …?	C'è … in questo piatto? Non lo posso
I'm not allowed to	mangiare. tshe … ēn kōō·e'stō pyä'tō?
eat that.	nōn lō pō'sō mänjä're.

? **Che cosa prende per *antipasto/*** Would you care for
dessert? ke kō'sä pren'de per *an appetizer/some*
äntēpä'stō/deser'? *dessert?*

No, thank you, ***L'antipasto/Il dessert non lo prendo,***
I don't care for *an* **grazie.** *läntēpä'stō/ēl deser'nōn lō*
appetizer/any dessert. pren'dō, grä'tsē·e.

INFO You can purchase entire cakes and tarts in the
pasticceria pästētsherē'ä. In restaurants you
can get single pieces of cakes for dessert.

| Could I have … | Potrei avere … invece di …? |
| instead of …? | pōtre'ē äve're … ēnve'tshe dē …? |

? **Come la vuole la bistecca?** How would you like
kō'me lä vōō·ō'le lä bēste'kä? your steak?

Rare. **Al sangue.** äl sän'gōō·e.

Medium. **Non troppo cotta, ma non al sangue.**
nōn trō'pō kō'tō, mä nōn äl sän'gōō·e.

Well-done. **Ben cotta.** ben kō'tä.

Could you bring **Per favore, mi porti ancora …**
me *another/some* per fävō're, mē pōr'tē änkō'rä …
more …, please?

112

COMPLAINTS

I didn't order this. I **Non ho ordinato questo, io volevo …**
wanted … nōn ō ōrdēnä'tō kōō·e'stō, ē'ō vōle'vō …

The … is/are missing. **Manca/Mancano ancora …**
män'kä/mänkä'nō änkō'rä …

INFO At the **bar** or **bar pasticceria** bär pästētsherē'ä
you can get a typically Italian breakfast: **cappuccino e brioche** käpōōtshē'nō e brē·ōsh' or
pasta pä'stä (a piece of cake or pastry). You can also get something small there for lunch. You must almost always pay for
your meal at the cashier's first; you must present your **scontrino**
skōntrē'nō (receipt) to get your meal or drink. Usually one eats
and drinks while standing at the counter. But in the summer, a
bar might put some tables outside. The prices will differ
according to whether you are eating at the counter or at a table
with service. A **bar gelateria** bär jelätere'ä will produce its own
ice cream; a **bar pasticceria** bär pästētsherē'ä offers its own
home-made cakes.

4

The meat hasn't been **La carne non è abbastanza cotta.**
cooked enough. lä kär'ne nōn e äbästän'tsä kō'tä.

Could you take it **Lo riporti indietro, per favore.**
back, please? lō rēpōr'tē ēndye'trō, per fävō're?

THE CHECK, PLEASE

Could I have the check, please?	**Il conto, per favore.** ēl kōn'tō, per fävō're.
I'd like a receipt.	**Vorrei la ricevuta.** vōre'ē lä rētshevōō'tä.
We'd like separate checks, please.	**Conti separati, per favore.** kōn'tē sepärä'tē, per fävō're.

INFO When Italians go out to eat with friends, they usually get one bill and figure out each one's share. Going Dutch is called **pagare alla romana** pägä're ä'lä rōmä'nä.

May I treat you?	*La/Ti* **posso invitare?** lä/tē pō'sō ēnvētä're?	
You're my guest today.	**Oggi** *è/sei* **mio ospite.** ō'jē *e/se'ē* mē'ō ō'spite.	
?	**È stato di** *Suo/vostro* **gradimento?** e stä'tō dē *sōō'ō/vōs'trō* grädēmen'tō?	Did you enjoy your meal?
It was very nice, thank you.	**Grazie, era davvero molto buono.** grä'tsē·e, e'rä däve'rō mōl'tō bōō·ō'nō.	
I think there must be some mistake here.	**Mi sembra che ci sia un errore.** mē sem'brä ke tshē sē'ä ōōn erō're.	

114

INFO The **birreria** bērerē'ä is only open in the evening. There you can get cold and sometimes simple warm dishes. These informal restaurants offer a large selection of beers. In general, beer in Italy is rather expensive, and imported beers are more expensive than Italian ones.

We didn't order this.	**Questo non lo abbiamo ordinato.** kōō·e'sto nōn lō äbyä'mō ōrdēnä'tō.
Thank you very much.	**Molte grazie.** mōl'te grä'tsē·e.

DINING WITH FRIENDS

Enjoy your meal!	**Buon appetito!** bōō·on' äpetē'tō!
Cheers!	**(Alla) salute!** (ä'lä) sälōō'te!
? *Le/Ti* piace? le/tē pyä'tshe?	How do you like it?
It's very good, thank you.	**È molto buono, grazie.** e mōl'tō bōō·ō'nō, grä'tsē·e.
That's exquisite.	**Questo è veramente squisito.** kōō·e'sto e verämen'te skōōēzē'tō.
What's that?	**Che cos'è?** ke kōse'?
Would you pass me the ..., please?	**Mi** *potrebbe/potresti* **passare ...?** mē *pōtre'be/pōtre'stē* päsä're ...?

4

Ancora un po' di …?
änkō'rä ōōn pō dē …?

Would you like some more?

Yes, please.

Sì, volentieri. sē, vōlentye'rē.

No, thanks, not right now.

Per il momento no, grazie. per ēl mōmen'tō nō, grä'tsē·e.

No, thank you, I'm full.

Grazie, ma sono già ♂ sazio/♀ sazia. grä'tsē·e, mä sō'nō jä ♂ sä'tsyō/♀ sä'tsyä.

Do you mind if I smoke?

La/Ti disturbo se fumo? lä/tē dēstōōr'bō sē fōō'mō?

Thank you for inviting me.

Grazie per l'invito. grä'tsē·e per lēnvē'tō.

It was delicious.

È stato eccellente. e stä'tō etshelen'te.

➡ see also: Please, Thank you (p. 25)

Food and drink

appetizer	**l'antipasto** läntēpä'sto
artificial sweetener	**il dolcificante** ēl dōltshēfēkän'te
ashtray	**il posacenere** ēl pōzätshe'nere
available	**libero** lē'berō
bar	**il bar** ēl bär
beer	**la birra** lä bē'rä
bottle	**la bottiglia** lä bōtē'lyä
– opener	**l'apribottiglie** *m* läprēbōtē'lye
bread	**il pane** ēl pä'ne

– roll	**il panino** ēl pänē'nō
whole-wheat –	**il pane integrale** ēl pä'ne ēntegrä'le
breakfast	**la colazione** lä kōlätsyō'ne
to bring	**portare** pōrtä're
butter	**il burro** ēl bōō'rō
café	**il bar, la pasticceria, il caffè** ēl bär, lä pästētsherēä, ēl käfe'
cake	**la torta** lä tōr'tä
carafe	**la caraffa** lä kärä'fä
cheese	**il formaggio** ēl fōrmä'jō
children's portion	**la mezza porzione** lä me'tsä pōrtsyō'ne
(hot) chocolate	**la cioccolata** lä tshōkōlä'tä
cocoa	**il cacao** ēl käkä'ō
coffee	**il caffè** ēl käfe'
black –	**il caffè nero** ēl käfe' ne'rō
decaffeinated –	**il caffè decaffeinato** ēl käfe' dekäfe-ēnä'tō
regular –	**il caffè alla tedesca** ēl käfe' ä'lä tedes'kä
– with milk	**il caffelatte, il caffè macchiato** ēl käfelä'te, ēl käfe' mäkyä'tō
– with sugar	**il caffè zuccherato** ēl käfe' tsōōkerä'tō
cold	**freddo** fre'dō
– cut platter	**l'affettato** läfetä'tō
cookies	**i biscotti** ē bēskō'tē
corkscrew	**il cavatappi** ēl kävätä'pē
course	**il piatto** ēl pyä'tō
first –	**il primo** ēl prē'mō

4

117

second –	**il secondo** ēl sekōn'dō
cream	**la panna** lä pä'nä
crudités	**le verdure crude** le verdōō're krōō'de
cup	**la tazza** lä tä'tsä
cutlery	**le posate** le pōsä'te
dessert	**il dolce** ēl dōl'tshe
diabetic	**il diabetico** ēl dyäbe'tēkō
diet	**la dieta** lä dē·e'tä
dinner	**la cena** lä tshe'nä
dish	**il piatto** ēl pyä'tō
dough	**la pasta** lä pä'stä
drink	**la bevanda** lä bevän'dä
to drink	**bere** be're
drinks menu	**la carta delle bevande** lä kär'tä de'le bevän'de
to eat	**mangiare** mänjä're
egg	**l'uovo,** *pl:* **le uova** lōō·ō'vō, *pl:* le ōō·ō'vä
fried –	**l'uovo al tegame** lōō·ō'vō äl tegä'me
hard-boiled –	**l'uovo sodo** lōō·ō'vō sō'dō
scrambled –	**le uova strapazzate** leōō·ō'vä sträpätsä'te
soft-boiled –	**l'uovo alla coque** lōō·ō'vō ä'lä kōk
excellent	**eccellente** etshelen'te
fat	**grasso** grä'sō
filling	**il ripieno** ēl rēpye'nō
fish	**il pesce** ēl pe'she
food	**il mangiare** ēl mänjä're

118

fork	**la forchetta**	lä forke'tä
fresh	**fresco**	fres'kō
fruit	**la frutta**	lä frōō'tä
to be full	**essere sazio**	e'sere sä'tsyō
garlic	**l'aglio**	(ä'lyō)
glass	**il bicchiere**	ēl bēkye're
grease	**il grasso**	ēl grä'sō
guest	**l'ospite** *m, f*	lō'spēte
ham	**il prosciutto**	ēl prōshōō'tō
hard	**duro**	dōō'rō
homemade	**fatto in casa**	fä'tō ēn kä'sä
honey	**il miele**	ēl mye'le
hot *(temperature)*	**caldo**	käl'dō
hot *(spicy)*	**piccante**	pēkän'te
to be hungry	**avere fame**	äve're fä'me
ice (cube)	**il (cubetto di) ghiaccio**	ēl (kōōbe'tō dē) gyä'tshō
to invite	**invitare**	ēnvētä're
jam	**la marmellata**	lä märmelä'tä
ketchup	**il ketchup**	ēl ket'shäp
knife	**il coltello**	ēl kōlte'lō
lean	**magro**	mäg'rō
light food	**gli alimenti dietetici**	lyē älēmen'tē dyete'tēshē
lunch	**il pranzo**	ēl prän'tsō
margarine	**la margarina**	lä märgärē'nä
mayonnaise	**la maionese**	lä mäyōne'ze
meat	**la carne**	lä kär'ne
menu	**il menù**	ēl menōō'

4

119

milk	**il latte** ēl läˈte
mineral water	**l'acqua minerale** läˈkōō·ä mēnerä'le
non-carbonated –	**l'acqua minerale naturale**
	läˈkōō·ä mēnerä'le nätōōrä'le
carbonated –	**l'acqua minerale gassata**
	läˈkōō·ä mēnerä'le gäsä'tä
mushrooms	**i funghi** ē fōōnˈgē
napkin	**il tovagliolo** ēl tōvälyō'lō
non-alcoholic	**analcolico** änälkō'lēkō
oil	**l'olio** lō'lyō
olive –	**l'olio d'oliva** lō'lyō dōlē'vä
onion	**la cipolla** lä tshēpō'lä
to order	**ordinare** ōrdēnä're
to pay	**pagare** pägä're
pepper	**il pepe** ēl pe'pe
peppermint tea	**l'infuso di menta** lēnfōō'zō dē men'tä
piece	**il pezzo** ēl pe'tsō
pizza	**la pizza** lä pē'tsä
place setting	**il coperto** ēl kōper'tō
place, seat	**il posto** ēl pō'stō
portion	**la porzione** lä pōrtsyō'ne
to recommend	**consigliare** kōnsēlyä're
to reserve	**prenotare** prenōtä're
restaurant	**il ristorante** ēl rēstōrän'te
restroom	**la toilette** lä tōō·älēt'
salad	**l'insalata** lēnsälä'tä
salt	**il sale** ēl sä'le
sandwich	**il panino (imbottito)**
	ēl pänē'nō (ēmbōtē'tō)

sauce *(in general)*	**la salsa** lä säl'sä
sauce *(for pasta)*	**il sugo** ēl sōō'gō
seasoned	**condito** kōndē'tō
to get separate checks	**pagare separatamente** pägä're sēpärätämen'te
slice	**la fetta** lä fe'tä
soft	**morbido** mōr'bēdō
soup *(in general)*	**la zuppa** lä tsōō'pä
soup *(with pasta or rice)*	**la minestra** lä mēnes'trä
sour *(culinary in general)*	**agro** ä'grō
sour *(of milk products)*	**acido** ä'tshēdō
special of the day	**il piatto del giorno** ēl pyä'tō del jōr'nō
speciality	**la specialità** lä spetshälētä'
spice	**le spezie** le spe'tsye
spoon	**il cucchiaio** ēl kōōkyä'yō
straw *(for drinking)*	**la cannuccia** lä känōō'tshä
sugar	**lo zucchero** lō tsōō'kerō
sweet	**dolce** dōl'tshe
table	**il tavolo** ēl tä'vōlō
to taste good	**piacere** pyätshe're
tea	**il tè** ēl te
camomile –	**la camomilla** lä kämōmē'lä
fruit –	**la tisana di frutta** lä tēzä'nä dē frōō'tä
–spoon	**il cucchiaino** ēl kōōkyä·ē'nō
tender	**tenero** ten'erō

4

121

to be thirsty	**avere sete** äve're se'te
tip	**la mancia** lä män'tshä
toast	**il toast** ēl tōst
vegetables	**la verdura** lä verdōō'rä
vegetarian	**vegetariano** vejetäryä'nō
vinegar	**l'aceto** lätshe'tō
waiter	**il cameriere** ēl kämerye're
waitress	**la cameriera** lä kämerye'rä
water	**l'acqua** lä'kōō·ä
wine	**il vino** ēl vē'nō
zwieback	**la fetta biscottata** lä fe'tä bēskōtä'tä

Sightseeing

TOURIST INFORMATION

May I have …

Vorrei … vōre′ē …

a list of hotels?

un annuario degli alberghi.
ōōn änōō-är′yō del′yē älber′gē.

a map of the area?

una cartina della zona.
ōō′nä kärtē′nä de′lä dzō′nä.

a brochure
about … ?

un depliant su …
ōōn deplē-än′ sōō …

a street map?

una pianta della città.
ōō′nä pyän′tä de′lä tshētä′.

a subway map?

una cartina della metropolitana.
ōō′nä kärtē′nä de′lä metrōpōlētä′nä.

a schedule of
events?

un programma delle manifestazioni.
ōōn prōgrä′mä de′le
mänēfestätsyō′nē

Could you reserve
a room for me?

Mi potrebbe prenotare una camera?
mē pōtre′be prenōtä′re ōō′nä kä′merä?

Are there *sightseeing
tours/guided walking
tours of the city?*

**Ci sono *giri turistici organizzati della
città/delle visite guidate*?** tshē sō′nō
jē′rē tōōrē′stētshē ōrgänēdzä′tē de′le ts-
hētä′/de′le vē′zēte gōō-ēdä′te?

How much does the
sightseeing tour cost?

**Quanto costa il biglietto per il giro
turistico della città?** kōō-än′tō kō′stä el
bēlye′tō per el jē′rō tōōrē′stēkō de′lä
tshētä′?

How long does the sightseeing tour last?	**Quanto dura il giro turistico della città?** kōō·än'tô dōō'rä ēl jē'rô tōōrē'stēkô de'lä tshētä'?
I'd like *a ticket/two tickets* for the walking tour of the city, please.	*Un biglietto/Due biglietti* **per la visita guidata, per favore.** ōōn bēlye'tô/dōō'e bēlye'tē per lä vē'zētä gōō·ēdä'tä, per fävō're.
I'd like to visit …	**Vorrei visitare …** vôre'ē vēzētä're …
Please reserve *a place/two places* on tomorrow's excursion for *me/us*.	*Un biglietto/Due biglietti* **per la gita di domani per** *me/noi,* **per favore.** ōōn bēlye'tô/dōō'e bēlye'tē, per lä jē'tä dē dômä'nē per *me/noē,* per fävō're.
Where/When do we meet?	*Dove/Quando* **ci troviamo?** kōō·än'dô/dô've tshē trôvyä'mô?
Will we also be visiting … ?	**Andiamo a vedere anche …?** ändyä'mô ä vede're än'ke …?
Will we also have some free time?	**Abbiamo tempo libero a disposizione?** äbyä'mô tem'pô lē'berô ä dēspōzētsyō'ne?
When do we start?	**A che ora si parte?** ä ke ô'rä sē pär'te?
When do we get back?	**A che ora ritorniamo?** ä ke ô'rä rētôrnyä'mô?

➡ *Hotel reservation: Accommodations (S. 34),*
Asking the way: On the Way (S. 54),
Public transportation: Bus, Subway, Taxi (S. 87)

5

SIGHTSEEING, EXCURSIONS

When is … *open/
closed*?

A che ora *apre/chiude* …?
ä ke ō'rä *ä'pre/kyōō'de* …?

What's the admission
charge?

Quanto costa il biglietto d'ingresso?
kōō·än'tō kō'stä ēl bēlye'tō dēngre'sō?

How much does the
guided tour cost?

Quanto costa la visita guidata?
kōō·än'tō kō'stä lä vē'zētä gōō·ēdä'tä?

Is there a discount
for …

C'è una riduzione per …
tshe ōō'nä rēdōōtsyō'ne per …

    families?
    groups?
    children?
    senior citizens?
    students?

    famiglie? fämē'lye?
    gruppi? grōō'pē
    bambini? bämbē'nē?
    anziani? ändzyä'nē?
    studenti? stōōden'tē?

INFO When visiting churches and monasteries, you should wear appropriate clothing (something that covers your shoulders and knees). It is possible that someone wearing shorts or something with an open neckline might not be allowed into the building.

Do you also have
tours in English?

C'è una guida che parla inglese?
tshe ōō'nä gōō·ē'dä ke pär'lä ēn·gle'se?

When does the tour
begin?

Quando inizia la visita guidata?
kōō·än'dō ēnē'tsyä lä vē'zēta gōō·ēdä'tä?

126

One ticket/ *Two tickets*, please.	**Un biglietto/Due biglietti, per favore.** ōōn bēlye'tō/dōō'e bēlye'tē, per fävo're.
Two adults and two children, please.	**Due adulti e due bambini, per favore.** dōō'e ädōōl'tē e dōō'e bämbē'nē, per fävo're.
Are you allowed to *take pictures/make a video*?	**Si possono fare *fotografie/delle riprese filmate*?** sē pō'sono fä're fōtōgräfē'e de'le rēpre'se fēlmä'te?
What *building/ monument* is that?	**Che *edificio/monumento* è questo?** ke edēfē'tshō/mōnōōmen'tō e kōō·e'stō?
When was ... built?	**Quando è stato costruito ...?** kōō·än'dō e stä'tō kōstrōō·ē'tō ...?
Do you have a *catalog/guide*?	**C'è *un catalogo/una guida*?** tshe ōōn kätä'lōgō/ōō'nä gōō·ē'dä?
Do you have a ... of that picture?	**Avete ... del quadro?** äve'tē ... del kōō·ä'drō?
slide	**una diapositiva** ōō'nä dē·äpōzētē'vä
poster	**un poster** ōōn pō'ster
postcard	**una cartolina** ōō'nä kärtōlē'nä

Sightseeing, Excursions

abbey	**l'abbazia** läbätsē'ä
alley	**il vicolo** ēl vē'kōlō
altar	**l'altare** *m* lältä're

5

127

amphitheater	**l'anfiteatro** länfētē·ä'trō
antique	**antico** äntē'kō
antiquity	**l'antichità** läntēkētä'
aqueduct	**l'acquedotto** läkōō·edō'tō
arcarde	**l'arcata** lärkä'tä
arch	**l'arco** lär'kō
archeological find	**i reperti archeologici** ē reper'tē ärke·ōlō'jētshē
archeology	**l'archeologia** lärke·ōlōje'ä
architect	**l'architetto** lärkēte'tō
architecture	**l'architettura** lärkētetōō'rä
area	**la zona** lä dzō'nä
arena	**l'arena** läre'nä
art	**l'arte** f lär'te
– collection	**la collezione di quadri** lä kōletsyō'ne dē kōō·ä'drē
artist	**l'artista** m, f lärtē'stä
atrium	**l'atrio** lä'trē·ō
avenue	**il viale** ēl vyä'le
baptismal font	**il fonte battesimale** ēl fōn'te bätezēmä'le
baroque	**il barocco** ēl bärō'kō
basilica	**la basilica** lä bäzē'lēkä
bell	**la campana** lä kämpä'nä
– tower	**il campanile** ēl kämpänē'le
bridge	**il ponte** ēl pōn'te
brochure	**il depliant** ēl deplē·än'
building	**la costruzione** lä kōstrōōtsyō'ne
bust	**il busto** ēl bōō'stō

128

Byzantine	**bizantino** bēdzäntē'nō	
capital	**la capitale** lä käpētä'le	
castle	**il castello** ēl käste'lō	
catacombs	**le catacombe** le kätäkōm'be	
cathedral	**la cattedrale, il duomo**	
	lä kätedrä'le, ēl dōō·ō'mō	
Catholic	**cattolico** kätō'lēkō	
cave	**la grotta** lä grō'tä	
ceiling	**il soffitto** ēl sōfē'tō	
cemetery	**il cimitero** ēl tshēmēte'rō	
century	**il secolo** ēl se'kōlō	
chapel	**la cappella** lä käpe'lä	
chimes	**il carillon** ēl kärēyōn'	
choir	**il coro** ēl kō'rō	
Christian	**cristiano** krēstyä'nō	
church	**la chiesa** lä kye'zä	
– service	**la messa** la me'sä	
city	**la città** lä tshētä'	
– center	**il centro** ēl tshen'trō	
– district	**il quartiere** ēl kōō·ärtye're	
– gate	**la porta della città**	
	lä pōrtä de'lä tshētä'	
– hall	**il municipio** ēl mōōnētshē'pyō	
historical part of the –	**il centro storico, la città vecchia**	
	ēl tshen'trō stō'rēkō, lä tshētä' ve'kyä	
map of the –	**la cartina della città**	
	lä kärtē'nä de'lä tshētä'	
– square	**la piazza** lä pyä'tsä	

5

129

– walls	**le mura (della città)**
	le mōō'rä (de'lä tshētä)
Classicism	**il classicismo** ēl kläsētshēz'mō
cloister	**il chiostro** ēl kyōs'trō
closed	**chiuso** kyōō'sō
coat-of-arms	**lo stemma** lō ste'mä
column	**la colonna** lä kôlô'nä
contemporary	**contemporaneo** kôntempōrä'ne·ō
convent	**il convento** ēl kônven'tō
copy	**la copia** lä kō'pyä
Corinthian	**corinzio** kōrēn'tsyō
court	**la corte** lä kôr'te
courtyard	**il cortile** ēl kōrtē'le
cross	**la croce** lä krō'tshe
crucifix	**il crocefisso** ēl krōtshefē'sō
crypt	**la cripta** lä krēp'tä
cupola	**la cupola** lä kōō'pōlä
Doric	**dorico** dō'rēkō
drawing	**il disegno** ēl dēzen'yō
emperor	**l'imperatore** lēmperätō're
empress	**l'imperatrice** lēmperätrē'tshe
era	**l'epoca** le'pōkä
Etruscan	**etrusco** etrōō'skō
excavations	**gli scavi** lyē skä'vē
excursion	**la gita** lä jē'tä
exhibition	**la mostra** lä mōs'trä
façade	**la facciata** lä fätshä'tä
forest	**il bosco** ēl bô'skō
fortress	**la fortezza** lä fōrte'tsä

130

fountain	**la fontana** lä fōntä'nä
fresco	**l'affresco** läfre'sko
gable	**il frontone, il timpano** ēl frōntō'ne, ēl tēm'pänō
garden	**il giardino** ēl järde'nō
gate	**la porta** lä pōr'tä
glass	**il vetro** ēl ve'trō
gorge	**la gola** lä gō'lä
Gothic	**gotico** gō'tēkō
Greek	**greco** gre'kō
Greeks	**i greci** ē gre'tshē
hall *(large room)*	**la sala** lä sä'lä
harbor	**il porto** ēl pōr'tō
hill	**la collina** lä kōlē'nä
history	**la storia** lä stōr'yä
inscription	**la scritta** lä skrē'tä
Ionic	**ionico** ē-ō'nēkō
island	**l'isola** lē'zōlä
king	**il re** ēl re
lake	**il lago** ēl lä'gō
landscape	**il paesaggio** ēl pä-ezä'jō
marble	**il marmo** ēl mär'mō
market	**il mercato** ēl merkä'tō
covered –	**il mercato coperto** ēl merkä'tō kōper'tō
Middle Ages	**il medioevo** ēl medyō-e'vō
model *(figurine)*	**il modello** ēl mōde'lō
modern	**moderno** mōder'nō
monastery	**il monastero** ēl mōnäste'rō

monument	**il monumento** ĕl mōnōōmen'tō	
mosaic	**il mosaico** ĕl mōzä'ēkō	
mountain	**la montagna** lä mōntän'yä	
mural	**la pittura murale** lä pētōō'rä mōōrä'le	
museum	**il museo** ĕl mōōze'ō	
folklore –	**il museo delle tradizioni popolari** ĕl mōōze'ō de'le trädētsyō'nē pōpōlä'rē	

national park	**il parco nazionale** ĕl pär'kō nätsēōnä'le	
nature preserve	**la zona protetta** lä dzō'nä prōte'tä	
open	**aperto** äper'tō	
opera	**l'opera** lō'perä	
organ	**l'organo** lōrgä'nō	
original	**l'originale** *m* lōrējēnä'le	
painter	**il pittore** ĕl pētō're	
painting	**il quadro** ĕl kōō·ä'drō	
palace	**il palazzo** ĕl pälä'tsō	
park	**il parco** ĕl pär'kō	
pedestrian zone	**la zona pedonale, la zona blu** lä dzō'nä pedōnä'le, lä dzō'nä blōō	
peninsula	**la penisola** lä penē'zōlä	
to take photographs	**fotografare** fōtōgräfä're	
picture	**il quadro** ĕl kōō·ä'drō	
pilgrim	**il pellegrino** ĕl pelegrē'nō	
pillar	**il pilastro** ĕl pēlä'strō	
(floor) plan	**la pianta** lä pyän'tä	
planetarium	**il planetario** ĕl plänetär'yō	
poet	**il poeta** ĕl po·e'tä	
porcelain	**la porcellana** lä pōrtshelä'nä	

132

portal	**il portale** ēl pōrtä'le
portrait	**il ritratto** ēl rēträ'tō
pottery	**l'arte della ceramica** lär'te de'lä tsherä'mēkä
queen	**la regina** lä rejē'nä
to reconstruct	**ricostruire** rēkōstrōō-ē're
relief	**il rilievo** ēl rēlēe'vō
religion	**la religione** lä relējō'ne
remains	**i resti** ē re'stē
Renaissance	**il Rinascimento** ēl rēnäshēmen'tō
to restore	**restaurare** restourä're
river	**il fiume** ēl fyōō'me
Roman	**romano** rōmä'nō
Romanesque	**romanico** rōmä'nēkō
Romans	**i romani** ē rōmä'nē
romantic	**romantico** rōmän'tēkō
ruin	**la rovina** lä rōvē'nä
sanctuary *(place of pilgrimage)*	**il santuario** ēl säntōō-är'yō
sandstone	**la pietra arenaria** lä pye'trä ärenär'yä
sarcophagus	**il sarcofago** ēl särkō'fägō
sculptor	**lo scultore** lō skōōltō're
sculpture	**la scultura** lä skōōltōō'rä
statue	**la statua** lä stä'tōō-ä
style	**lo stile** lō stē'le
surrounding area	**i dintorni** ē dēntōr'nē
synagogue	**la sinagoga** lä sēnägō'gä
temple	**il tempio** ēl tem'pyō
theater	**il teatro** ēl te-ä'trō

5

133

tomb	**la tomba** lä tōmb'bä
tour of the city/town	**la visita guidata della città** lä vē'zētä gōō·ēdä'tä de'lä tshētä'
tourist information office	**l'ufficio informazioni turistiche** lōōfē'tshō ēnfōrmätsyō'nē tōōrē'stēke
tower	**la torre** lä tō're
treasure chamber	**il tesoro** ēl tesō'rō
triumphal arch	**l'arco di trionfo** lär'kō dē trē·ōn'fō
university	**l'università** lōōnēversētä'
valley	**la valle** lä vä'le
vase	**il vaso** ēl vä'zō
vault	**la volta** lä vōl'tä
to videotape	**filmare** fēlmä're
view	**il panorama** ēl pänōrä'mä
vineyard	**il vigneto** ēl vēnye'tō
to visit	**visitare** vēzētä're
volcano	**il vulcano** ēl vōōlkä'nō
wall	**il muro** ēl mōō·rō
waterfall	**la cascata** lä käskä'tä
window	**la finestra** lä fēne'strä
wine-tasting	**la degustazione del vino** lä degōōstätsyō'ne del vē'nō
wing	**l'ala** lä'lä
woodcarving *(as a handicraft)*	**l'intaglio** lēntä'lyō
woodcarving *(figure)*	**la scultura in legno** lä skōōltōō'rä en le'nyō
work	**l'opera** lō'perä
zoo	**lo zoo** lō dzō'ō

134

INFO In Italy there are a great many wildlife preserves that protect rare animal and plant species. There are bears and wolves in the **Parco Nazionale degli Abruzzi** pär'kō nätsyōnä'le de'lyē äbrōō'tsē. The **Parco del Pollino** pär'kō del pōlē'nō is wellknown for its rare plant forms.

Plants

almond tree	**il mandorlo** ēl män'dōrlō
beech tree	**il faggio** ēl fä'jō
broom	**la ginestra** lä jēnes'trä
chestnut tree	**il castagno** ēl kästä'nyō
cork oak tree	**il sughero** ēl sōō'gerō
cypress tree	**il cipresso** ēl tshēpre'sō
grape vines	**le viti** le vē'tē
larch tree	**il larice** ēl lä'rētshe
lemon tree	**il limone** ēl lēmō'ne
maritime pine tree	**il pino marittimo** ēl pē'nō märē'tēmō
oak tree	**la quercia** lä kōō·er'tshä
oleander	**l'oleandro** lōle·än'drō
olive tree	**l'ulivo** lōōlē'vō
orange tree	**l'arancio** lärän'tshō
spruce tree	**il pino** ēl pē'nō
stone/umbrella pine tree	**il pino a ombrello** ēl pē'nō ä ōmbre'lō
walnut tree	**il noce** ēl nō'tshe

5

135

Animals

boar	**il cinghiale** ēl tshēn·gyä'le
butterfly	**la farfalla** lä färfä'lä
cat	**il gatto** ēl gä'tō
cow	**la mucca** lä mōō'kä
dog	**il cane** ēl kä'ne
donkey	**l'asino** lä'sēnō
eagle	**l'aquila** lä'kōō-ēlä
fox	**la volpe** lä vōl'pe
horse	**il cavallo** ēl kävä'lō
ibex *(mountain goat)*	**lo stambecco** lō stämbe'kō
mule	**il mulo** ēl mōō'lō
snake	**la serpe, il serpente** lä ser'pe, ēl serpen'te
wolf	**il lupo** ēl lōōpō

Shopping

BASIC PHRASES

Where can I get …?	**Dove posso trovare …?** dōve pō'sō trōvä're …	
! **Dica, prego!** dē'kä, pre'gō!		May I help you?
? **Posso aiutarLa?** pō'sō äyōōtär'lä?		May I help you?

I'm just looking, thanks.

Grazie, ma vorrei soltanto dare un'occhiata. grä'tsē-ē, mä vōre'ē sōltän'tō dä're ōōnōkyä'tä.

I'm being helped, thanks.

Mi stanno già servendo. mē stä'nō jä serven'dō.

I'd like …

Vorrei … vōre'ē …

Please give me …

Per favore, mi dia … per fävō're, mē dē'ä …

a can of …

un barattolo (in general)/**una lattina** (drink) **di …** ōōn bärä'tōlō/ōō'nä lätē'nä dē …

a bottle of …

una bottiglia di … ōō'nä bōtē'lyä dē …

a jar of …

un barattolo di … ōōn bärä'tōlō dē …

a package of …

un pacco di … ōōn pä'kō dē …

a box of …

una scatola di … ōō'nä skä'tōlä dē …

a tube of …

un tubetto di … ōōn tōōbe'tō dē …

! **Mi dispiace, ma … è finito.** mē dēspyä'tshe, mä … e fēnē'tō.

I'm sorry, but we're out of …

| How much is/are ...? | **Quanto costa/costano ...?** |
| | kōō·än'tō *kō'stä/kō'stäno* ...? |

| Could you show me ..., please? | **Per favore, mi fa vedere ...?** |
| | per fävō're, mē fä vede're ...? |

| That's not quite what I'm looking for. | **Questo non mi piace tanto.** |
| | kōō·e'stō nōn mē pyä'tshe tän'tō. |

| Could you show me something else? | **Mi può mostrare qualcos'altro?** |
| | mē pōō·ō' mōsträ're kōō·älkōsäl'trō? |

| I'd like something a little less expensive. | **Vorrei qualcosa di meno caro.** |
| | vōre'ē kōō·älkō'sä de me'nō kä'rō. |

| I'll have to think about it. | **Ci devo pensare ancora un po'.** |
| | tshē de'vō pensä're änkō'rä ōōn pō. |

| I like this. I'll take it. | **Mi piace, lo prendo.** |
| | mē pyä'tshe, lō pren'dō. |

? **Desidera altro?** dese'derä äl'trō? Will there be anything else?

| That's all, thank you. | **Grazie, è tutto.** grä'tsē·e, e tōō'tō. |

| Can I pay with this credit card? | **Posso pagare con questa carta di credito?** pō'sō pägä're kōn kōō·e'sta kär'tä dē kre'dētō? |

| May I have a (plastic) bag for it? | **Ha un sacchetto (di plastica), per favore?** ä ōōn säke'tō (dē plä'stēkä), per fävō're? |

INFO When you buy something, you should make sure you get the **scontrino fiscale** sköntrë'nö fëskä'le (receipt) and hold on to it at least until you are 100 meters away from the store. In order to avoid tax evasion, the **Guardia di Finanza** gōō·är'dyä dē fēnän'tsä (finance police) has the right to check and make sure that the bill has been added up accurately. The **scontrino** is the proof that the owner of the store has registered his earnings properly. If you are not in possession of the **scontrino**, you could be fined as well.

Could you wrap it up well for my return trip, please?	**Me lo può incartare bene per il viaggio?** me lö pōō·ò' ēnkärtä're be'ne per ēl vyä'jō?
How much does it cost?	**Quanto costa?** kōō·än'tö kö'stä?
This is broken. Could you repair it?	**È rotto, lo può riparare?** e rö'tö, lö pōō·ò' rēpärä're?
When will it be ready?	**Per quando sarà pronto?** per kōō·än'dō särä' prön'tö?
I'd like to *exchange/return* this.	**Lo vorrei *cambiare/dare indietro*.** lö vöre'ē *kämbyä're/dä're ēndye'trö*.
I'd like a refund, please.	**Vorrei riavere indietro i soldi.** vöre'ē rē·äve're ēndye'trö ē söl'dē.
Sorry, but you haven't given me enough change. I'm short …	**Mi ha dato …. di meno.** mē ä dä'tö … dē me'nö.

General Vocabulary

(plastic) bag	**il sacchetto (di plastica)** ĕl säke'tō (dē plä'stëkä)
better	**migliore** mēlyō're
big	**grande** grän'de
bigger	**più grande** pyŏŏ grän'de
to buy	**comprare** kōmprä're
can	**la lattina** lä läte'nä
cheaper	**meno caro** me'nō kä'rō
to cost	**costare** kōstä're
credit card	**la carta di credito** lä kär'tä dē kre'dētō
to exchange	**cambiare** kämbyä're
expensive	**caro** kä'rō
gift	**il regalo** ĕl regä'lō
to give	**dare** dä're
money	**i soldi** ē sōl'dē
pack	**il pacchetto** ĕl päke'tō
package	**il pacco** ĕl pä'kō
receipt	**la ricevuta** lä rētshevōō'tä
to return	**dare indietro** dä're ĕndye'trō
self-service	**il self-service** ĕl self-ser'vĕs
to show	**mostrare** mōsträ're
small	**piccolo** pē'kōlō
smaller	**più piccolo** pyŏŏ pē'kōlō
special offer	**l'offerta speciale** lōfer'tä spetshä'le
to take	**prendere** pren'dere
too	**troppo** trō'pō
(shop) window	**la vetrina** lä vetrē'nä

Colors and Patterns

beige	**beige** *(inv)* bej
black	**nero** ne'rō
blue	**blu** *(inv)* blōō
brown	**marrone** märō'ne
checked	**a quadri** ä kōō·ä'drē
colorful	**colorato** kōlōrä'tō
dark	**scuro** skōō'rō
gold	**dorato** dōrä'tō
gray	**grigio** grē'jō
green	**verde** ver'de
light	**chiaro** kyä'rō
light blue	**azzurro** ädzōō'rō
patterned	**fantasia** fäntäze'ä
pink	**rosa** *(inv)* rō'zä
purple	**lilla** *(inv)* lē'lä
red	**rosso** rō'sō
silver	**argentato** ärjentä'tō
solid *(color)*	**in tinta unita** ēn tēn'tä ōōnē'tä
striped	**a righe** ä rē'ge
white	**bianco** byän'kō
yellow	**giallo** jä'lō

INFO Stores in Italy are generally open from 8:30 or 9 a.m. to 1 p.m., and then again from 4:30 or 5:30 p.m. to 8 p.m. In many towns grocery stores are closed on Thursday afternoons, and hairdressers and clothing stores are closed on Mondays.

6

Stores

antique store	**il negozio di antiquariato** ēl nĕgō'tsyō dē äntēkōō-äryä'tō
bakery	**la panetteria, il forno** lä pänĕtĕrē'ä, ēl fōr'nō
barbershop	**il barbiere** ēl bärbyē're
bookstore	**la libreria** lä lēbrĕrē'ä
butcher's	**la macelleria** lä mätshĕlĕrē'ä
clothing store	**il negozio di abbigliamento** ēl nĕgō'tsyō dē äbēlyämĕn'tō
confectionery	**la pasticceria** lä pästētshĕrē'ä
dairy store	**la latteria** lä lätĕrē'ä
department store	**il grande magazzino** ēl grän'de mägätsē'nō
drugstore	**la drogheria** lä drōgĕrē'ä
dry cleaner's	**la lavanderia a secco** lä lävändĕrē'ä ä se'kō
fish store	**la pescheria** lä peskĕrē'ä
florist's	**il fioraio** ēl fyōrä'yō
vegetable store	**il negozio di frutta e verdura** ēl nĕgō'tsyō dē frōō'tä e verdōō'rä

143

grocery store	**il negozio di generi alimentari**
	ēl negŏ'tsyō dē jen'erē älēmentä'rē
beauty shop	**il parrucchiere** ēl pärōōkye're
jewelry store	**la gioielleria** lä jōyelerē'ä
kiosk	**il chiosco** ēl kyō'skō
laundromat	**la lavanderia a gettone**
	lä lävänderē'ä ä jetō'ne
green market	**il mercato** ēl merkä'tō
music store	**il negozio di dischi** ēl negŏ'tsyō dē dē'skē
newsstand	**il giornalaio** ēl jōrnälä'yō
optician's	**l'ottico** lō'tēkō
perfume store	**la profumeria** lä prōfōōmerē'ä
camera store	**il negozio di articoli fotografici**
	ēl negŏ'tsyō dē ärtē'kōlē fōtōgrä'fētshē
shoe store	**il negozio di calzature**
	ēl negŏ'tsyō dē kältsätōō're
shoe-repair shop	**il calzolaio** ēl kältsōlä'yō
souvenir store	**il negozio di souvenir**
	ēl negŏ'tsyō dē sōōvenēr'
sporting-goods store	**il negozio di articoli sportivi**
	ēl negŏ'tsyō dē ärtē'kōlē spōrtē've
stationery store	**la cartoleria** lä kärtōlerē'ä
houseware store	**il negozio di casalinghi**
	ēl negŏ'tsyō dē käsälēn'gē
leather goods	**la pelletteria** lä peleterē'ä
supermarket	**il supermercato** ēl sōōpermerkä'tō
tobacconist's	**la tabaccheria** lä täbäkerē'ä

FOOD

What's that?	**Che cos'è quello?** ke kōse' kōō-e'lō?
Could I have …, please?	**Per favore, mi dia …** per fävō're, mē dē'ä …
100 grams of …	**un etto di …** ōōn e'tō dē …
250 grams of …	**due etti e mezzo di …** dōō'e e'tē e me'tsō dē …
a pound *(500 grams)* of …	**mezzo chilo di …** me'tsō kē'lō dē …
a kilo of …	**un chilo di …** ōōn kē'lō dē …
a slice of …	**una fetta di …** ōō'nä fe'tä dē …
a piece of …	**un pezzo di …** ōōn pe'tsō dē …
a serving of …	**una porzione di …** ōō'nä pōrtsyō'ne dē …
half a liter of …	**mezzo litro di …** me'tsō lē'trō dē …
A little *less/more*, please.	**Un po' di *meno/più*, per favore.** ōōn pō dē *me'nō/pyōō*, per fävō're.
May I try some (of that), please?	**Lo posso assaggiare?** lō pō'sō äsäjä're?

INFO   Normal bread in central Italy (**il filone di pane** ēl fēlō'ne dē pä'ne) is made without salt. Recently most places also offer **pane integrale** pä'ne ēntegrä'le (whole-wheat bread), **pane di segale** pä'ne dē se'gäle (rye bread), and breads made of various kinds of grains (**pane ai cinque cereali** pä'ne ī tshēn'kōō·e tshere·ä'lē). **Panini all'olio** pänē'nē älō'lēō are small, soft rolls that are particularly good for sandwiches.

apple	**la mela** lä me'lä
– juice	**il succo di mele** ēl sōō'kō dē me'le
apricot	**l'albicocca** lälbēkō'kä
artichoke	**il carciofo** ēl kärtshō'fō
artificial sweetener	**il dolcificante** ēl dōlshēfēkän'te
avocado	**l'avocado** lävōkä'dō
baby food	**gli alimenti per la prima infanzia** lyē älēmen'tē per lä prē'mä ēnfän'tsyä
banana	**la banana** lä bänä'nä
basil	**il basilico** ēl bäzē'lēkō
beans	**i fagioli** ē fäjō'lē
broad –	**i fagioli bianchi** ē fäjō'lē byän'kē
green –	**i fagiolini** ē fäjōlē'nē
beef	**la carne di manzo** lä kär'ne dē män'tsō
beer	**la birra** lä bē'rä
non-alcoholic –	**la birra analcolica** lä bē'rä änälkō'lēkä
bread	**il pane** ēl pä'ne
– roll	**il panino** ēl pänē'nō
whole-wheat –	**il pane integrale** ēl pä'ne ēntegrä'le
broccoli	**i broccoli** ē brō'kōlē
butter	**il burro** ēl bōō'rō
cabbage	**il cavolo** ēl kä'vōlō
cake	**la torta** lä tōr'tä
canned goods	**lo scatolame** lō skätōlä'me
cheese	**il formaggio** ēl fōrmä'jō
cherries	**le ciliege** le tshēlye'je
chicken	**il pollo** ēl pō'lō

(hot) chocolate	**la cioccolata** lä tshōkōlä'tä
chop	**la cotoletta** lä kōtōle'tä
cocoa	**il cacao** ēl käkä'ō
coffee	**il caffè** ēl käfe'
cold cuts	**l'affettato** läfetä'tō
cookies	**i biscotti** ē bēskō'tē
corn	**il mais** ēl mä'ēs
cream	**la panna** lä pä'nä
cucumber	**il cetriolo** ēl tshetrē-ō'lō
cutlet	**la cotoletta** lä kōtōle'tä
dates	**i datteri** ē dä'terē
egg	**l'uovo,** *pl:* **le uova** lōō-ō'vō, *pl:* le ōō-ō'vä
eggplant	**la melanzana** lä meläntsä'nä
figs	**i fichi** ē fē'kē
fish	**il pesce** ēl pe'she
fruit	**la frutta** lä frōō'tä
garlic	**l'aglio** lä'lyō
grapes	**l'uva** lōō'vä
ground meat	**la carne macinata** lä kär'ne mätshēnä'tä
ham	**il prosciutto** ēl prōshōō'tō
boiled –	**il prosciutto cotto** ēl prōshōō'tō kō'tō
cured –	**il prosciutto crudo** ēl prōshōō'tō krōō'dō
honey	**il miele** ēl mye'le
jam	**la marmellata** lä märmelä'tä
juice	**il succo** ēl sōō'kō
ketchup	**il ketchup** ēl ke'tshäp
kiwi fruit	**il kiwi** ēl kē'uē
lamb	**la carne d'agnello** lä kär'ne dänye'lō

leek	**il porro** ēl pō′rō
lemon	**il limone** ēl lēmō′ne
lettuce	**la lattuga** lä lätōō′gä
margarine	**la margarina** lä märgärē′nä
mayonnaise	**la maionese** lä mäyōne′se
meat	**la carne** lä kär′ne
melon	**il melone** ēl melō′ne
milk	**il latte** ēl lä′te
skim –	**il latte scremato** ēl lä′te skremä′tō
mineral water	**l'acqua minerale** lä′kōō·ä mēnerä′le
nectarine	**la pescanoce** lä peskänō′tshe
nuts	**le noci** le nō′tshe
(rolled) oats	**i fiocchi d'avena** ē fyōkē däve′nä
oil	**l'olio** lō′lēō
olive	**l'oliva** lōlē′vä
– oil	**l'olio d'oliva** lō′lēō dōlē′vä
onion	**la cipolla** lä tshēpō′lä
orange	**l'arancia** lärän′tshä
– juice	**il succo d'arancia**
	ēl sōō′kō därän′tshä
oregano	**l'origano** lōrē′gänō
parsley	**il prezzemolo** ēl pretsemō′lō
pasta	**la pasta** lä pä′stä
pistachios	**i pistacchi** ē pēstä′kē
peach	**la pesca** lä pe′skä
peas	**i piselli** ē pēse′lē
pepper *(spice)*	**il pepe** ēl pe′pe
pepper *(vegetable)*	**il peperone** ēl peperō′ne
pineapple	**l'ananas** *m* länänäs′

148

pork	**la carne di maiale**	lä kär'ne dē mäyä'le
potatoes	**le patate**	le pätä'te
poultry	**il pollame**	ēl pōlä'me
raspberries	**i lamponi**	ē lämpō'nē
rice	**il riso**	ēl rē'sō
salami	**il salame**	ēl sälä'me
salt	**il sale**	ēl sä'le
sandwich	**il panino imbottito**	ēl pänē'nō ēmbōtē'tō
sausages	**le salsicce**	le sälsē'tshe
soft drink	**la gassosa**	lä gäsō'sä
spices	**le spezie**	le spe'tsye
steak	**la bistecca**	lä bēste'kä
strawberries	**le fragole**	le frä'gōle
sugar	**lo zucchero**	lō tsōō'kerō
tangerine	**la clementina**	lä klementē'nä
tea	**il tè**	ēl te
tomato	**il pomodoro**	ēl pōmōdō'rō
tuna	**il tonno**	ēl tō'nō
veal	**la carne di vitello**	lä kär'ne dē vēte'lō
vegetables	**la verdura**	lä verdōō'rä
vinegar	**l'aceto**	lätshe'tō
watermelon	**il cocomero**	ēl kōkō'merō
wine	**il vino**	ēl vē'nō
red –	**il vino rosso**	ēl vē'nō rō'so
white –	**il vino bianco**	ēl vē'nō byän'kō
yogurt	**lo yogurt**	lō yō'gōōrt
zucchini	**le zucchine**	le tsōōkē'ne
zwieback	**la fetta biscottata**	lä fe'tä bēskōtä'tä

SOUVENIRS

What's typical of this area? | **Che cosa c'è di tipico in questa zona?** ke kō´sä tshe dē tē´pēkō ēn kōō-e·stä dzō´nä?

Is this handmade? | **È fatto a mano?** e fä´tō ä mä´nō?

Is this *antique/ genuine*? | **È *antico/autentico*?** e äntē´kō/outen´tēkō?

Souvenirs

arts and crafts	**l'artigianato artistico** lärtējänä´tō ärte´stēkō
belt	**la cintura** lä tshēntōō´rä
Capodimonte porcelain	**la (porcellana) capodimonte** lä (pōrtshelä´nä) käpōdēmōn´te
ceramics	**la ceramica** lä tsherä´mēkä
copper pot	**il paiolo di rame** ēl päyō´lō dē rä´me
crafts	**l'artigianato** lärtējänä´tō
doily	**il centrino** ēl tshentrē´nō
genuine	**autentico** outen´tēkō
glass	**il vetro** ēl ve´trō
goblet	**il calice** ēl kä´lētshe
handbag	**la borsa** lä bōr´sä
handmade	**fatto a mano** fä´tō ä mä´nō
jewelry	**i gioielli** ē jōye´lē
lace	**il pizzo** ēl pē´tsō
leather	**la pelle** lä pe´le
plate *(for hanging on the wall)*	**il piatto murale** ēl pyä´tō mōōrä´le

150

rug	**il tappeto** ēl täpe'tō
shoulder bag	**la borsa a tracolla** lä bōr'sä ä träkō'lä
souvenir	**il souvenir** ēl sŏŏvenēr'
statuette	**la statuetta** lä stätŏŏ·e'tä
straw hat	**il cappello di paglia** ēl käpe'lō dē päl'yä
terracotta	**la terracotta** lä teräkō'tä
typical	**tipico** tē'pēkō

CLOTHES AND DRY CLEANER'S

I'm looking for … **Vorrei …** vōre'ē …

? Che taglia porta? ke tä'lyä pōr'tä?   What size are you?

I'm a size … **Ho la taglia …** ō lä tä'lyä …

Do you also have this in a size … ? **Ha anche la taglia …?** ä än'ke lä tä'lyä …?

Do you have this in another color? **Ce l'ha anche di un altro colore?** tshe lä än'ke dē ōōn äl'trō kōlō're?

May I try this on? **Lo posso provare?** lō pō'sō prōvä're?

Where is the mirror? **Dov'è uno specchio?** dōve' ōō'nō spe'kyō?

What kind of material is this made of? **Di che materiale è?** dē ke mäteryä'le e?

It doesn't fit. **Non mi sta bene.** nōn mē stä be'ne.

151

It's too *big/small*.	**È troppo *grande/piccolo*.**	e trŏ'pō grän'de/pē'kōlŏ.
This fits perfectly.	**Questo va bene.** kōō-e'stō vä be'ne.	
I'd like this dry-cleaned.	**Vorrei far lavare a secco questo.** vōre'ē fär lävä're ä se'kō kōō-e'sto.	
Can you get rid of this stain?	**Può togliere questa macchia?** pōō-ō' tŏlye're kōō-e'stä mä'kyä?	

Clothes and Dry Cleaners

belt	**la cintura** lä tshēntōō'rä
blazer	**il blazer** ēl ble'zä
blouse	**la camicetta** lä kämētshe'tä
bra	**il reggiseno** ēl rejēse'nō
cap	**il berretto** ēl bere'tō
coat	**il cappotto** ēl käpō'tō
collar	**il collo** ēl kō'lō
color	**il colore** ēl kōlō're
cotton	**il cotone** ēl kōtō'ne
dress	**il vestito** ēl vestē'tō
to dry-clean	**lavare a secco** lävä're ä se'kō
elegant	**elegante** elegän'te
to fit	**stare bene** stä're be'ne
gloves	**i guanti** ē gōō-än'tē
hat	**il cappello** ēl käpe'lō
jacket	**la giacca** lä jä'kä
jeans	**i jeans** ē jēnz
leather	**la pelle** lä pe'le

152

linen	**il lino** ēl lē'nō
long	**lungo** lōōn'gō
material	**il materiale** ēl mäteryä'le
nightgown	**la camicia da notte** lä kämē'tshä dä nō'te
pajamas	**il pigiama** ēl pējä'mä
panties	**lo slip** lō slēp
pants	**i pantaloni** ē päntälō'nē
pantyhose	**il collant** ēl kōlän'
permanent press	**non-stiro** nōn-stē'rō
scarf *(silky)*	**il foulard** ēl fōōlär'
scarf *(woolen)*	**la sciarpa** lä shär'pä
shirt	**la camicia** lä kämē'tshä
short	**corto** kōr'tō
shorts	**gli shorts** lyē shōrts
silk	**la seta** lä se'tä
size	**la taglia** lä tä'lyä
skirt	**la gonna** lä gō'nä
sleeves	**le maniche** le mä'nēke
long –	**le maniche lunghe** le mä'nēke lōōn'ge
short –	**le maniche corte** le mä'nēke kōr'te
socks	**i calzini** ē kältsē'nē
stockings	**le calze** le käl'tse
sun hat	**il cappello da sole** ēl käpe'lō dä sō'le
sweater	**il maglione** ēl mälyō'ne
sweatpants	**i pantaloni della tuta** ē päntälō'nē de'lä tōō'tä
sweatsuit	**la tuta da ginnastica** lä tōō'tä dä jēnä'stēkä

6

T-shirt	**la maglietta** lä mälye'tä
terry cloth	**la spugna** lä spōō'nyä
tie	**la cravatta** lä krävä'tä
to try on	**provare** prōvä're
underpants	**le mutande** le mōōtän'de
Windbreaker®	**la giacca a vento** lä jä'kä ä ven'tō
wool	**la lana** lä lä'nä

➡ see also: Word list General Vocabulary (p. 141),
Word list Colors and Patterns (p. 142)

SHOES

I'd like a pair of …   **Vorrei un paio di …**
                         vōre'ē ōōn pä'yō dē …

? **Che numero di scarpe ha?**   What is your shoe
ke nōō'merō dē skär'pe ä?   size?

My size is …   **Ho il numero …** ō ēl nōō'merō …

The heel is too   **Il tacco è troppo *alto/basso*.**
high/low for me.   ēl tä'kō e trō'pō *äl'tō/bä'sō*.

They're too   **Sono troppo *grandi/piccole*.**
big/small.   sō'nō trō'pō *grän'dē/pē'kōle*.

They're too tight   **Mi fanno male qui.** mē fä'nō mä'le
around here.   kōō-ē'.

| Would you fix the heels, please? | **Mi rifaccia i tacchi, per favore.** mē rēfä'tshä ē tä'kē, per fävo're. |
| Could you re-sole the shoes, please? | **Me le può risuolare, per favore?** me le pōō·o' rēsōō·olä're, per fävo're? |

Shoes

boots	**gli stivali** lyē stēvä'lē
thongs	**le scarpette da bagno** le skärpe'tē dä bä'nyō
heel	**il tacco** ēl tä'kō
hiking boots	**le scarpe da escursioni** le skär'pe dä eskōōrsyō'nē
leather	**il cuoio** ēl kōō·o'yō
– sole	**la suola di cuoio** lä sōō·o'lä dē kōō·o'yō
mountain climbing boots	**gli scarponi da montagna** lyē skärpo'nē dä montä'nyä
pair	**il paio** ēl pä'yō
pumps	**le scarpe decolleté** le skärpe dekōlte'
rubber sole	**la suola di gomma** lä sōō·o'lä dē go'mä
sandals	**i sandali** ē sändä'lē
shoe polish	**il lucido da scarpe** ēl lōō'tshēdō dä skär'pe
shoelaces	**i lacci per le scarpe** ē lä'tshē per le skär'pe
shoes	**le scarpe** le skär'pe
size	**il numero** ēl nōō'merō
sneakers	**le scarpe da ginnastica** le skär'pe dä jēnä'stēkä

WATCHES AND JEWELRY

My watch is
fast/slow.

Il mio orologio va *avanti/indietro*.
ēl mē'ō ōrōlō'jō vä ävän'tē/ēndye'trō.

I'm looking for a nice
souvenir/present.

Vorrei un bel ricordino/regalo.
vōre'ē ōōn bel rēkōrdē'nō/regä'lō.

❓ Quanto vuole spendere?
kōō·an'tō vōō·ō'le spen'dere?

How much would
you like to pay?

What's this made of?

Di che materiale è? dē ke mäteryä'le e?

Watches and Jewelry

alarm clock	**la sveglia**	lä sve'lyä
battery	**la pila**	lä pē'lä
bracelet	**il bracciale**	ēl brätshä'le
brass	**l'ottone**	lōtō'ne
brooch	**la spilla**	lä spē'la
chain	**la catenina**	lä kätenē'nä
clip-on earrings	**gli orecchini a clip**	
	lyē ōreke'nē ä klēp	
costume jewelry	**la bigiotteria**	lä bējōterē'ä
earrings	**gli orecchini**	lyē ōreke'nē
gold	**l'oro**	lō'rō
gold-plated	**placcato in oro**	pläkä'tō ēn ō'rō
jewelry	**i gioielli**	ē jōye'lē
necklace	**la collana**	lä kōlä'nä
pendant	**il ciondolo**	ēl tshōn'dōlō
ring	**l'anello**	läne'lō

silver	**l'argento** lärjen'tō
silver-plated	**placcato in argento**
	pläkä'tō ēn ärjen'tō
watch	**l'orologio** lōrōlō'jō
–band	**il cinturino** ēl tshēntōōre'nō

PERSONAL HYGIENE AND HOUSEHOLD

INFO In Italy there is nothing exactly like the drug-stores in America. You will find some things in the **drogheria** drōgerē'ä. Otherwise you can purchase articles for personal hygiene and for infant care at the **farmacia** färmätshē'ä (pharmacy), and soaps and other cosmetic articles in the **profu-meria** profōōmerē'ä (perfume store) or at the supermarket.

Personal Hygiene

aftershave	**il dopobarba** ēl dōpōbär'bä
baby bottle	**il biberon** ēl bēberōn!
– nipple	**la tettarella** lä tetäre'lä
baby oil	**l'olio emolliente** lō'lēō emōlyen'te
baby powder	**il borotalco** ēl bōrōtäl'kō
barrette	**il fermaglio per i capelli**
	ēl fermä'lyō per ē käpe'lē
bath and shower gel	**il gel per la doccia**
	ēl jel per lä dō'tshä
bib	**il bavaglino** ēl bävälyē'nō
blusher	**il fard** ēl färd

157

body lotion	**la lozione per il corpo**	
	lä lōtsyō'ne per ēl kōr'pō	
brush	**la spazzola** lä spä'tsōlä	
cleansing cream	**il latte detergente** ēl lä'te deterjen'te	
comb	**il pettine** ēl pe'tēne	
condoms	**i profilattici, i preservativi**	
	ē prōfēlä'tētshē, ē preservätē'vē	
cotton	**il cotone idrofilo** ēl kōtō'ne ēdrō'fēlō	
– pads	**i dischetti uso cosmetico**	
	ē dēske'tē ōō'zō kōsme'tēkō	
deodorant	**il deodorante** ēl de·ōdōrän'te	
detergent	**il detersivo** ēl detersē'vō	
diapers	**i pannolini** ē pänōlē'nē	
eye shadow	**l'ombretto** lōmbre'tō	
fragrance-free	**non profumato** nōn prōfōōmä'tō	
hair drier	**l'asciugacapelli** *m* läshōōgäkäpe'lē	
hair-styling gel	**il gel per capelli** ēl jel per käpe'lē	
hair-styling mousse	**la schiuma (fissante)**	
	lä skyōō'mä (fēsän'te)	
hairband	**l'elastico per i capelli**	
	lelä'stēkō per ē käpe'lē	
hairspray	**la lacca** lä lä'kä	
handcream	**la crema per le mani**	
	lä kre'mä per le mä'nē	
handkerchief	**il fazzoletto** ēl fatsōle'tō	
lip balm	**il burro cacao** ēl bōō'rō käkä'ō	
lipstick	**il rossetto** ēl rōse'tō	
mascara	**il mascara** ēl mäskä'rä	
mirror	**lo specchio** lō spe'kyō	

158

mosquito repellent	**il fornellino antizanzare**	
	ēl fōrnelē'nō äntēdzändzä're	
nail file	**la limetta per le unghie**	
	lä lēme'tä per le ōōn'gye	
nail polish	**lo smalto per le unghie**	
	lō zmäl'tō per le ōōn'gye	
– remover	**il solvente per lo smalto**	
	ēl sōlven'te per lō zmäl'tō	
nail scissors	**le forbici per le unghie**	
	le fōr'bētshē per le ōōn'gye	
pacifier	**il succhietto** ēl sōōkye'tō	
paper towels	**gli asciugamani usa e getta**	
	lyē äshōōgämä'nē ōō'zä e je'tä	
perfume	**il profumo** ēl prōfōō'mō	
pH-balanced	**pH-neutro** pē-ä'kä-ne'ōōtrō	
plaster	**il cerotto** ēl tsherō'tō	
powder	**la cipria** lä tshēp'rē-ä	
razor	**il rasoio** ēl räsō'yō	
– blade	**la lametta** lä läme'tä	
sanitary napkins	**gli assorbenti igienici**	
	lyē äsōrben'tē ēje'nētshē	
shampoo	**lo shampoo** lō shäm'pō	
skin cream	**la crema per la pelle**	
	lä kre'mä per lä pe'le	
– for dry skin	**la crema per pelli secche**	
	lä kre'mä per pe'lē se'ke	
– for oily skin	**la crema per pelli grasse**	
	lä kre'mä per pe'lē grä'se	
soap	**la saponetta** lä säpōne'tä	

SPF (sun protection factor)	**il fattore di protezione** ĕl fätō're dē prōtetsēō'ne
suntan cream	**la crema solare** lä kre'mä sōlä're
suntan gel	**il gel solare** ĕl jel sōlä're
suntan lotion	**il latte solare** ĕl lä'te sōlä're
tampons	**i tamponi** ē tämpō'nē
tissues	**i fazzoletti da strucco, – di carta** ē fätsōle'tē dä strōō'kō dē kär'tä
toilet paper	**la carta igienica** lä kär'tä ēje'nēkä
toothbrush	**lo spazzolino da denti** lō spätzōlē'nō dä den'tē
toothpaste	**il dentifricio** ĕl dentēfrē'tshō
towel	**l'asciugamano** läshōōgämä'nō
tweezers	**le pinzette** le pēntse'tē
washcloth	**il guanto di spugna** ĕl gōō·än'tō dē spōō'nyä

Household

adapter	**l'adattatore** m lädätätō're
alarm clock	**la sveglia** lä zve'lyä
aluminum foil	**il foglio di alluminio** ĕl fō'lyō dē älōōmē'nyō
battery	**la pila** lä pē'lä
bottle opener	**l'apribottiglie** m läprēbōtē'lye
broom	**la scopa** lä skō'pä
bucket	**il secchio** ĕl se'kyō
can opener	**l'apriscatole** m läprēskä'tōle
candle	**la candela** lä kände'lä

160

charcoal	**la carbonella** lä kärböne'lä	
cleaning products	**il detersivo** ēl detersē'vō	
clothes line	**il filo per stendere i panni**	
	ēl fē'lō per sten'dere ē pä'nē	
clothes pins	**le mollette (per i panni)**	
	le mōle'te (per ē pä'nē)	
corkscrew	**il cavatappi** ēl kävätä'pē	
cup	**la tazza** lä tä'tsä	
paper –	**il bicchiere di carta**	
	ēl bēkye're dē kär'tä	
detergent	**il detersivo** ēl detersē'vō	
dish-washing liquid	**il detersivo per le stoviglie**	
	ēl detersē'vō per le stōve'lye	
dishcloth	**lo strofinaccio** lō strōfēnä'tshō	
extension cord	**la prolunga** lä prōlōōn'gä	
flashlight	**la lampada tascabile**	
	lä läm'pädä täskä'bēle	
fork	**la forchetta** lä fōrke'tä	
gas cartridge	**la cartuccia per il fornellino a gas**	
	lä kärtōō'tshä per ēl fōrnelē'nō ä gäs	
glass	**il bicchiere** ēl bēkye're	
grill	**il grill** ēl grēl	
knife	**il coltello** ēl kōlte'lō	
light bulb	**la lampadina** lä lämpädē'nä	
lighter	**l'accendino** lätshendē'nō	
matches	**i fiammiferi** ē fyämē'ferē	
mosquito net	**la zanzariera** lä dzändzärye'rä	
napkins	**i tovaglioli** ē tōvälyō'lē	
pan	**la padella** lä päde'lä	

plastic cutlery	**le posate di plastica** le pōsä'te de plä'stēkä
plate	**il piatto** ēl pyä'tō
paper –	**i piatti di carta** ē pyä'tē dē kär'tä
pocket knife	**il coltello tascabile** ēl kōlte'lō täskä'bēle
pot	**la pentola** lä pen'tōlä
safety pin	**lo spillo da balia** lō spē'lō dä bä'lyä
scissors	**le forbici** lē fōr'bētshē
scrubbing brush	**lo spazzolone** lō spätsōlō'ne
sewing needle	**l'ago** lä'gō
solid fire lighter	**l'accendifuoco** lätshendēfōō-ō'kō
spoon	**il cucchiaio** ēl kōōkyä'yō
string	**lo spago** lō spä'gō
thread	**il filo da cucito** ēl fē'lō dä kōōtshē'tō
toothpick	**lo stuzzicadenti** lō stōōtsēkäden'tē

AT THE OPTICIAN'S

My glasses are broken.	**Mi si sono rotti gli occhiali.** mē sē sō'nō rō'tē lyē ōkyä'lē.
Can you fix this?	**Me lo può aggiustare?** me lō pōō-ō' äjōōstä're?
I'm *nearsighted/ farsighted.*	**Sono *miope/presbite.*** sō'nō mē'ōpe/prez'bēte.

I'd like a pair of *sunglasses/prescription sunglasses*.	**Vorrei un paio di occhiali *da sole/da vista con filtro solare.*** vō're'ē ōōn pä'yō dē ōkyä'lē dä sō'le/dä vē'stä kōn fēl'trō sōlä're.
I've *lost/broken* a contact lens.	***Ho perso/Mi si è rotta* una lente a contatto.** ō per'sō/mē sē e rō'tä ōō'nä len'te ä kōntä'tō.
I need some *rinsing/cleaning* solution for *hard/soft* contact lenses.	**Ho bisogno di una soluzione *per la conservazione/detergente* per lenti a contatto *rigide/morbide.*** ō bēzō'nyō dē ōō'nä sōlōōtsyō'ne per lä kōnservätsēō'ne/deterjen'te per len'tē ä kōntä'tō rē'jēde/mōr'bēde.

6

AT THE HAIRDRESSER'S

I'd like to make an appointment for ...	**Vorrei un appuntamento per ...** vō're'ē ōōn äpōōntämen'tō per ...
? Che cosa deve fare? ● ke kō'sä de've fä're?	What would you like to have done?
Just a trim, please.	**Soltanto il taglio.** sōltän'tō ēl tä'lyō.
I'd like it washed, cut and blow-dried, please.	**Taglio, shampoo e fon, per favore.** tä'lyō, shäm'pō e fōn, per fävō're.
? Come vuole tagliarli? ● kō'me vōō-ō'le tälyär'lē?	How do you want it cut?

I'd like ...	**Vorrei ...** vōre'ē
a perm.	**una permanente.** ōō'nä permänen'te.
some highlights put in.	**farmi le mèche.** fär'mē le mesh.
to have a color rinse.	**dei riflessi.** de'ē rēfle'sē.

Not too short, please.	**Non troppo corti, per favore.** nōn trō'pō kōr'tē, per fävō're.

A little shorter, please.	**Un po' più corti, per favore.** ōōn pō pyōō kōr'tē, per fävō're.

Could you make the ... a bit shorter, please?	**Li sfoltisca un po' ..., per favore.** lē sfōltē'skä ōōn pō ..., per fävō're.
back	**dietro** dye'trō
front	**davanti** dävän'tē
sides	**ai lati** ī lä'tē
top	**sopra** sō'prä

Part it on the *left/right*, please.	**Faccia la riga a *sinistra/destra*, per favore.** fä'tshä lä rē'gä ä *sēnēs'trä/des'trä*, per fävō're.

Please trim my beard.	**Mi tagli la barba, per favore.** mē tä'lyē lä bär'bä, per fävō're.

Please give me a shave.	**La barba, per favore.** lä bär'bä, per fävō're.

bangs	**la frangetta** lä fränje'tä
beard	**la barba** lä bär'bä
black	**nero** ne'rō
blond(e)	**biondo** byōn'dō
to blow-dry	**asciugare con il fon** äshōōgä're kōn ēl fōn
chestnut (brown)	**castano** kästä'nō
color rinse	**il riflessante** ēl rēflesän'te
to cut	**tagliare** tälyä're
dandruff	**la forfora** lä fōr'fōrä
to dye	**tingere** tēn'jere
hair	**i capelli** ē käpe'lē
– cut	**il taglio** ēl tä'lyō
dry –	**i capelli secchi** ē käpe'lē se'kē
oily –	**i capelli grassi** ē käpe'lē grä'sē
– spray	**la lacca** lä lä'kä
– style	**la pettinatura** lä petēnätōō'rä
highlights	**le mèche** le mesh
moustache	**i baffi** ē bä'fē
part *(in hair)*	**la riga** lä rē'gä
perm	**la permanente** lä permänen'te
razor cut	**il taglio con il rasoio** ēl tä'lyō kōn ēl räsō'yō
to set in curlers	**mettere in piega** me'tere ēn pye'gä
shampoo	**lo shampoo** lō shäm'pō
to shave	**fare la barba** fä're lä bär'ba
to wash	**lavare** lävä're

PHOTO AND VIDEO

I'd like …

    a roll of film for this camera.

    a *color/black-and-white* film.

    a slide film.

    a *24/36* exposure film.

    a …ASA film.

    a VHS video cassette.

I'd like some batteries for this camera.

Could you please put the film in for me?

I'd like to get this film developed.

Vorrei … vōre'ē

    una pellicola per questa macchina fotografica. ōō'na pelē'kōlä per kōō-e'stä mä'kēnä fōtōgrä'fēkä.

    una pellicola *a colori/in bianco e nero.* ōō'nä pelē'kōlä ä kōlō'rē/ēn byän'kō e ne'rō.

    una pellicola per diapositive. ōō'nä pelē'kōlä per dē-äpōzētē've.

    una pellicola da *ventiquattro/trentasei* pose. ōō'nä pelē'kōlä dä veniēkōō-ä'trō/trentäse'ē pō'se.

    una pellicola da … ASA. ōō'nä pelē'kōlä dä … ä'sä.

    una videocassetta VHS. ōō'nä vēde-ōkäse'tä vōō-ä'kä-e'se.

Vorrei delle pile per questa macchina fotografica. vōre'ē de'le pē'le per kōō-e'stä mä'kēnä fōtōgrä'fēkä.

Mi potrebbe inserire la pellicola, per favore? mē pōtre'be ēnserē're lä pelē'kōlä, per fävō're?

Vorrei far sviluppare questo rullino. vōre'ē fär zvēlōōpä're kōō-e'stō rōōlē'nō.

Just develop the negatives, please.	**Soltanto le negative, per favore.**	
	sŏltän'tŏ le negätē've, per fävŏ're.	
I'd like a … x … picture from each negative, please.	**Una stampa di ogni negativa, formato … per …, per favore.**	**6**
	ōō'na stäm'pä dē ŏ'nyē negätē'vä, formä'tŏ … per …, per fävŏ're.	

? Lucido od opaco? Glossy or silk finish?
lōō'tshēdŏ ŏd ŏpä'kŏ?

When will the pictures be ready?	**Quando saranno pronte le foto?**
	kōō·än'dŏ särä'nŏ prŏn'te le fŏ'tŏ?
Could you repair my camera?	**Mi potrebbe riparare la macchina fotografica?**
	mē pŏtre'be rēpärä're lä mä'kēnä fŏtŏgrä'fēkä?
The film doesn't wind forward.	**La pellicola non scorre.**
	lä pelē'kŏlä nŏn skŏ're.
The *shutter release/ flash* doesn't work.	**Lo scatto/Il flash non funziona.**
	lŏ skä'tŏ/ēl flesh nŏn fōōntsyŏ'nä.
I'd like to have passport photos taken.	**Vorrei farmi delle foto formato tessera.**
	vŏre'ē fär'mē de'le fŏ'tŏ fŏrmä'tŏ te'serä.
Do you have any … by …?	**Avete … di …?** äve'te … dē …?
CD's	**dei compact disc**
	de'ē kŏm'päkt dēsk
cassettes	**delle cassette** de'lē käse'te
records	**dei dischi** de'ē dē'skē

167

| Do you have the latest cassette by … | **Vorrei l'ultima cassetta di …** vôre'ĕ lōōl'tĕmä käse'tä dĕ … |
| I'm interested in folk music. What would you recommend? | **Mi interessa molto la musica tradizio-nale. Potrebbe consigliarmi qualcosa?** mē ēntere'sä mōl'tō lä mōō'zĕkä trädĕtsyōnä'le. pōtre'be kōnsēlyär'mē kōō·älkō'sä? |

Photo and Video

automatic shutter	**l'autoscatto** loutōskä'tō
battery	**la pila** lä pē'lä
camera	**la macchina fotografica** lä mä'kēnä fōtōgrä'fēkä
cassette	**la cassetta** lä käse'tä
CD	**il compact disc** ēl kōm'päkt dēsk
to develop	**sviluppare** zvēlōōpä're
to expose	**esporre** espō're
film	**la pellicola** lä pelē'kōlä
black-and-white –	**la pellicola in bianco e nero** lä pelē'kōlä ēn byän'kō e ne'rō
color –	**la pellicola a colori** lä pelē'kōlä ä kōlō'rē
slide –	**la pellicola per diapositive** lä pelē'kōlä per dē·äpōzētē've
to film	**filmare** fēlmä're
flash	**il flash** ēl flesh
lens	**l'obiettivo** lōbyetē'vō
light meter	**l'esposimetro** lespōzēm'etrō
movie camera	**la cinepresa** lä tshēnepre'sä

music	**la musica** lä mōō´zēkä
negative	**il negativo** ēl negätē´vō
picture	**la foto** lä fō´tō
radio	**la radio** lä rä´dyō
record *(LP)*	**il disco** ēl dē´skō
shutter	**lo scatto** lō skä´tō
slide	**la diapositiva** lä dē·äpōzētē´vä
UV filter	**il filtro UV** ēl fē´ltrō ōō-vē´
VHS	**VHS** vōō-ä´kä-e´se
video-8	**il video-8** ēl vē´de-ō-ō´tō
videocamera	**la videocamera** lä vēde-ōkä´merä
videocassette	**la videocassetta** lä vēde-ōkäse´tä
Walkman®	**il Walkman®** ēl vōōk´men
wide-angle lens	**il grandangolare** ēl grändän-gōlä´re
zoom lens	**il teleobiettivo** ēl tele-ōbyetē´vō

READING AND WRITING

I'd like …

    an *American/ English* news- paper.

    an *American/ English* magazine.

    a map of the area.

Vorrei … vōre´ē …

    un giornale *americano/inglese.* ōōn jōrnä´le ämerēkä´nō/ēn-gle´se.

    una rivista *americana/inglese.* ōō´nä rēvē´stä ämerēkä´nä/en-gle´se.

    una cartina di questa zona. ōō´nä kärtē´nä dē kōō·e´stä dzō´nä.

Do you have a more current issue?	**Ha anche un giornale più recente?**
Do you have any books in English?	ä än'ke ōōn jōrnä'le pyōō retshen'te?
	Avete anche dei libri in inglese?
	äve'te än'ke de'ē lē'brē ēn ēn·gle'se?
Do you have stamps?	**Si possono comprare anche i francobolli qui?** sē pō'sōnō kōmprä're än'ke ē fränkōbō'lē kōō·ē'?

Reading and Writing

adhesive tape	**il nastro adesivo** ēl näs'trō ädeze'vō
ball-point pen	**la penna a sfera** lä pe'nä ä sfe'rä
board game	**il gioco di società** ēl jō'kō dē sōtsh·etä'
book	**il libro** ēl lē'brō
color pencil	**la matita colorata** lä mätē'tä kōlōrä'tä
coloring book	**l'album** *m* **da colorare** läl'bōōm dä kōlōrä're
cookbook	**il libro di cucina** ēl lē'brō dē kōōtshē'nä
dictionary	**il dizionario** ēl dētsyōnär'yō
drawing pad	**l'album** *m* **da dissegno** läl'bōōm dä dēse'nyō
envelope	**la busta** lä bōō·stä
eraser	**la gomma per cancellare** lä gō'mä per käntshelä're
felt-tip pen	**il pennarello** ēl penäre'lō
glue	**la colla** lä kō'lä
ink cartidges	**le cartucce per la stilografica** le kärtōō'tshe per lä stēlōgrä'fēkä
magazine	**la rivista** lä rēvē'stä

170

map	**la carta** lä kär'tä
– of bicycle routes	**la carta dei percorsi ciclabili** lä kär'tä de'ē perkôr'sē tshēklä'bēlē
city –	**la cartina della città** lä kärtē'nä de'lä tshētä'
– of hiking trails	**la carta dei percorsi escursionistici** lä kär'tä de'ē perkôr'sē eskōōrsyōnē'stētshē
newspaper	**il giornale (quotidiano)** ēl jōrnä'le (kōō-ōtēdyä'nō)
note pad	**il bloc-notes** ēl blōk-nō'tes
novel	**il romanzo** ēl rōmän'tsō
detective –	**il giallo** ēl jä'lō
paper	**la carta** lä kär'tä
airmail –	**la carta da lettere per posta aerea** lä kär'tä dä le'tere per pō'stä ä-e're·ä
pencil	**la matita** lä mätē'tä
– sharpener	**il temperamatite** ēl temperämätē'te
picture book	**il libro illustrato** ēl lē'brō ēlōōsträ'tō
playing cards	**le carte da gioco** le kär'te dä jō'kō
postcard	**la cartolina** lä kärtōlē'nä
road map	**la carta stradale** lä kär'tä strädä'le
stamp	**il francobollo** ēl fränkōbō'lō
travel guide	**la guida** lä gōō-ē'dä
wrapping paper	**la carta da regalo** lä kär'tä dä regä'lō
writing paper	**la carta da lettere** lä kär'tä dä le'tere

6

AT THE TOBACCONIST'S

Do you have any
American cigarettes?

Ha sigarette americane?
ä sēgäre'te ämerēkä'ne?

A pack of ...,
filtered/unfiltered
cigarettes, please.

Un pacchetto di sigarette *con/senza*
filtro, per favore. ōōn päke'tō dē
sēgäre'te *kōn/sen'tsä* fēl'trō, per fävō're.

INFO You can purchase cigarettes in the **tabaccheria**
täbäkerē'ä (tobacconist's) and in bars desig-
nated as a **bar tabaccheria** bär täbäkerē'ä by a blue sign with a
white "T." You can also get stamps in either of these.

A pack/A carton
of ..., please.

Un pacchetto/Una stecca di ..., per
favore. ōōn päke'tō/ōō'nä ste'kä dē ...,
per fävō're.

A package of ...
pipe/cigarette
tobacco, please.

Un pacchetto di tabacco *da pipa/per*
sigarette, per favore. ōōn päke'tō dē
täbä'kō *dä pē'pä/per sēgäre'te*, per
fävō're.

Could I have *a box of*
matches/a lighter,
please?

Una scatola di fiammiferi/Un
accendino, per favore. ōō'nä skä'tōlä dē
fyämē'ferē/ōōn ätshende'nō, per fävō're.

Entertainment and Sports

SWIMMING AND WATER SPORTS

At the Beach

Is there a beach nearby?	**C'è una spiaggia qui vicino?** tshe ōō'nä spyä'jä kōō-ē' vētshē'no?
How do you get to the beach?	**Come si arriva alla spiaggia?** kō'me sē ärē'vä ä'lä spyä'jä?

INFO In Italy there are **spiagge private** spyä'je prēvä'te (private beaches) which you may not use because they belong to private citizens or hotels. The **stabilimenti balneari** stäbēlēmen'tē bälne·ä'rē are sections of beach that are watched over and cleaned privately or by companies. If you wish to visit one of these beaches, you are required to rent a space with an umbrella and a lounge chair. Only the **spiagge libere** spyä'je lē'bere (public beaches) may be used at no cost.

Is there any shade there?	**C'è un po' d'ombra?** tshē ōōn pō dōm'brä?
How *deep*/*warm* is the water?	**Quant'è *alta*/*calda* l'acqua?** kōō·änte' *äl'tä/käl'dä* lä'kōō·ä?
Are there strong currents here?	**Ci sono delle correnti?** tshē sō'nō de'le kōren'tē?
Is it dangerous for children?	**È pericoloso per i bambini?** e perēkōlō'sō per ē bämbē'nē?

Are there jellyfish around here?	**Ci sono meduse?** tshē sō'nō medōō'ze?
Where can I rent …?	**Dove si può noleggiare …?** dō've sē pōō·ō' nōlejä're …?
I'd like to rent a *lounge chair/beach umbrella.*	**Vorrei noleggiare *una sedia a sdraio/un ombrellone.*** vōre'ē nōlejä're ōō'nä se'dyä ä zdrä'yō/ōōn ōmbrelō'ne.
I'd like to go waterskiing.	**Vorrei fare dello sci acquatico.** vōre'ē fä're de'lō shē äkōō·ä'tēkō.
I'd like to take *scuba diving/windsurfing* lessons.	**Vorrei fare un corso di *nuoto subacqueo/surf.*** vōre'ē fä're ōōn kōr'sō dē nōō·ō'tō sōōbäkōō·e'ō/serf.
Would you keep an eye on my things for a moment, please?	**Per favore, starebbe attento alle mie cose per un attimo?** per fävō're, stäre'be äten'tō ä'le mē'e kō'se per ōōn ä'tēmō?

7

At the Swimming Pool

Is there an *indoor/ outdoor* pool nearby?	**C'è una piscina *all'aperto/coperta* qui vicino?** tshe ōō'nä pēshē'nä äläper'tō/ kōper'tä kōō·ē vētshē'nō?
How much does it cost to get in?	**Quanto costa il biglietto d'ingresso?** kōō·än'tō kō'stä ēl bēlye'tō dēngre'sō?
What coins do I need for the *lockers/ hair-dryers?*	**Che monete ci vogliono per *gli armadietti/ l'asciugacapelli?*** ke mōne'te tshē vōl'yōnō per lyē ärmädye'tē/läshōōgäkäpe'lē?

175

Is there also a sauna here?	**C'è anche la sauna?** tshe än'ke lä sou'nä?
I'd like to rent ...	**Vorrei noleggiare ...** vōre'ē nōlejä're ...
a bathing cap.	**una cuffia.** ōō'nä kōō'fyä.
a towel.	**un asciugamano.** ōōn äshōōgämä'nō.
some water wings.	**dei braccioli salvagente.** de'ē brätshä'lē sälväjen'te.
Where's the *lifeguard/ first-aid station*?	**Dov'è il *bagnino/posto di pronto soccorso*?** dōve' ēl bänyē'no/pō'stō dē prōn'tō sōkōr'sō?

Swimming and Water Sports

air mattress	**il materassino pneumatico** ēl mäteräsē'nō pnē-ōōmä'tēkō
bathing cap	**la cuffia** lä kōō'fyä
bathing suit	**il costume da bagno** ēl kōstōō'me dä bä'nyō
beach	**la spiaggia** lä spyä'jä
– umbrella	**l'ombrellone** lōmbrelō'ne
bikini	**il bikini** ēl bēkē'nē
boat	**la barca** lä bär'kä
– rental	**il noleggio di barche** ēl nōle'jō dē bär'ke
calm	**calmo** käl'mō
changing room	**la cabina** lä käbē'nä
current	**la corrente** lä kōren'te
dangerous	**pericoloso** perēkōlō'sō
deckchair	**la sedia a sdraio** lä se'dyä ä zdrä'yō

176

diving board	**il trampolino** ēl trämpōlē'nō	
diving gear	**l'equipaggiamento da sub** lekōō-ēpäjämen'tō dä sōōb	
to go fishing	**pescare** peskä're	
fishing boat	**il peschereccio** ēl peskere'tshō	
flippers	**le pinne** le pē'ne	
heated spa	**il bagno termale** ēl bä'nyō termä'le	
inflatable boat	**il canotto pneumatico** ēl känō'tō pne-ōōmä'tēkō	
jellyfish	**la medusa** lä medōō'zä	
lifesaver	**il salvagente** ēl sälväjen'te	
motorboat	**il motoscafo** ēl mōtōskä'fō	
non-swimmer	**i non nuotatori** ē nōn nōō-ōtätō're	
nudist beach	**la spiaggia per nudisti** lä spyä'jä per nōōdē'stē	
outdoor pool	**la piscina all'aperto** lä pēshē'nä äläper'tō	
pedal boat	**il pattino a pedali** ēl pätē'nō ä pedä'lē	
rocks *(large)*	**gli scogli** *m/pl* lyē skōlyē	
rough *(sea)*	**mosso** mō'sō	
rowboat	**la barca a remi** lä bär'kä ä re'mē	
to go sailing	**praticare la vela** prätēkä're lä ve'lä	
sailboat	**la barca a vela** lä bär'kä ä ve'lä	
sand	**la sabbia** lä sä'byä	
sandy beach	**la spiaggia con la sabbia** lä spyä'jä kōn lä sä'byä	
sauna	**la sauna** lä sou'nä	
to go scuba diving	**fare nuoto subacqueo** fä're nōō-ō'tō subä'kōō-ō	
sea	**il mare** ēl mä're	

– urchin	**il riccio di mare** ēl rē'tshō dē mä're
shade	**l'ombra** lōm'brä
shells	**le conchiglie** le kōnkē'lye
shower	**la doccia** lä dō'tshä
snorkel	**il respiratore** ēl respērätō're
storm warning	**il segnale di tempesta**
	ēl senyä'le dē tempe'stä
surfboard	**la tavola da surf** lä tä'vōlä dä serf
to go swimming	**nuotare** nōō-ōtä're
(as a sport)	
to go swimming	**fare il bagno** fä're ēl bä'nyō
(for pleasure)	
swimming pool	**la piscina** lä pēshē'nä
swimming trunks	**il costume da bagno** ēl kōstōō'me dä bä'nyō
tide	**la marea** lä märe'ä
high –	**l'alta marea** läl'tä märe'ä
low –	**la bassa marea** lä bä'sä märe'ä
towel	**l'asciugamano** läshōōgämä'nō
water	**l'acqua** lä'kōō-ä
– polo	**la pallanuoto** lä pälänōō-ō'tō
– skiing	**lo sci acquatico** lō shē äkōō-ä'tēkō
– wings	**i bracciali salvagente**
	ē brätshä'lē sälväjen'te
wave	**l'onda** lōn'dä
wet suit	**la tuta subacquea** lä tōō'tä sōōbä'kōō-ä
wicker beach chair	**la poltroncina da spiaggia**
	lä pōltrōntshē'nä dä spyä'jä
wind-surfing school	**la scuola di surf** lä skōō-ō'lä dē serf

MOUNTAINEERING

I'd like to take a … hour hike.
Vorrei fare un'escursione di … ore.
vōre'ē fä're ōōneskōōrsyō'ne dē … ō're.

I'd like to *go to/climb* …
Vorrei andare *a/su* …
vōre'ē ändä're *ä/sōō* …

Can you recommend *an easy/a moderately difficult* hiking trail?
Mi può consigliare un percorso *piuttosto facile/di media difficoltà?*
mē pōō·ō' kōnsēlyä're ōōn perkōr'sō *pyōōt'stō fä'tshēle/dē me'dyä dēfēkōltä'?*

Approximately how long will it take?
Quanto tempo ci vuole all'incirca?
kōō·än'tō tem'pō tshē vōō·ō'le älentshēr'kä?

Is the path *well marked/secure*?
L'itinerario è ben *indicato/sicuro*?
lētēnerär'yō e ben *ēndēkä'tō/sēkōō'rō*?

Is there anywhere we can get something to eat along the way?
C'è un luogo di ristoro lungo il percorso? tshe ōōn lōō·ō'gō dē rēstō'rō lōōn'gō ēl perkōr'sō?

Are there guided tours?
Ci sono escursioni guidate?
tshē sō'nō eskōōrsyō'nē gōō·ēdä'te?

When does the *next/last* cable car go *up/come down*?
A che ora parte *la prossima/l'ultima* funivia per *salire/scendere*? ä ke ō'rä pär'te *lä prō'sēmä/lōōl'tēmä* fōōnēvē'ä per *sälē're/shen'dere*?

| Is this the right way to …? | **Siamo sulla strada giusta per …?** |
| | syä'mō sōō'lä strä'dä jōō'stä per …? |

| How much farther is it to …? | **Quanto manca per arrivare a …?** |
| | kōō·än'tō män'kä per ärēvä're ä …? |

| I'm not afraid of heights. | **Non soffro di vertigini.** |
| | nōn sō'frō dē vertē'jēnē |

Mountaineering

cable car	**la funivia** lä fōōnēvē'ä
chair lift	**la seggiovia** lä sejōvē'ä
hike	**l'escursione** *f* leskōōrsyō'ne
to go hiking	**fare escursioni** fä're eskōōrsyō'nē
hiking boots	**le scarpe da escursione**
	le skär'pe dä eskōōrsyō'ne
hiking map	**la carta dei sentieri**
	lä kär'tä de'ē sentye'rē
hiking trail	**il sentiero** ēl sentye'rō
hut	**il rifugio** ēl rēfōō'jō
mountain	**la montagna** lä mōntä'nyä
– climbing	**l'alpinismo** lälpēnēz'mō
– guide	**la guida alpina** lä gōō·ē'dä älpē'nä
mountain-climbing boots	**gli scarponi da montagna**
	lyē skärpō'nē dä mōntä'nyä
provisions	**le provviste** *f/pl* le prōv'ēste
ravine	**la gola** lä gō'lä
rope	**la corda** lä kōr'dä

SKIING

I'd like to …

Vorrei … vōre'ē …

enroll my *son/daughter* for skiing lessons.

iscrivere *mio figlio/mia figlia* al corso di sci. ēskrē'vere mē'ō fē'lyō/mē'ä fē'lyä äl kôr'sō dē shē.

take a skiing course.

fare un corso di sci. fä're ōōn kôr'sō dē shē.

have a private instructor.

prendere un maestro di sci. pren'dere ōōn mä-estrō dē she.

I'd like to rent …

Vorrei noleggiare … vōre'ē nōlejä're …

cross-country skis.

un paio di sci da fondo. ōōn pä'yō dē shē dä fôn'dō.

cross-country skiing boots, size …

un paio di scarpette da sci di fondo numero … ōōn pä'yō dē skärpe'te dä'shē dē fôn'dō nōō'merō …

downhill skis.

un paio di sci da discesa. ōōn pä'yō dē shē dä dēshe'sä.

downhill skiing boots, size …

un paio di scarponi da sci numero … ōōn pä'yō dē skärpō'nē dä shē nōō'merō …

a snowboard.

uno snowboard. ōō'nō snō'bôrd.

ice skates, size …

un paio di pattini numero … ōōn pä'yō dē pä'tēnē nōō'merō …

a sled.

una slitta. ōō'nä slē'tä.

I'm …	**Sono …** sō'nō …
a beginner.	**♂ un principiante / ♀ una princi-piante.** ♂ ōōn prēntshēpyän'te/ ♀ ōō'nä prēntshēpyän'te.
an average skiier.	**uno sciatore piuttosto mediocre.** ōōn'nō shē·äto're pyōōtō'stō medyō'kre.
a good skiier.	**un bravo sciatore.** ōōn brä'vō shē·äto're.
I'd like a lift pass for …	**Vorrei uno ski-pass per …** vōre'ē ōō'nō ske'päs per …
a half-day.	**mezza giornata.** me'tsä jōrnä'tä.
a day.	**un giorno.** ōōn jōr'nō.
two days.	**due giorni.** dōō'e jōr'nē.
a week.	**una settimana.** ōō'nä setēmä'nä.

> **❗ Ci vuole una fotografia formato tessera.** tshē vōō·ō'le ōō'nä fōtōgräfē'ä fōrmä'tō te'serä.
>
> You'll need a passport photo.

Where can I get a passport photo made?	**Dove posso fare delle fotografie formato tessera?** dō've po'sō fä're de'le fōtōgräfē'e fōrmä'tō te'serä?
When is the half-day pass valid?	**Da che ora è valido lo ski-pass per mezza giornata?** dä ke ō'rä e vä'lēdō lō ske'päs per me'tsä jōrnä'tä?
When is the last downhill run?	**A che ora c'è l'ultima discesa a valle?** ä ke ō'rä tshe lōōl'tēmä dēshe'sä ä vä'le?

When do the lifts *start/stop* running?	**Da/Fino a che ora funziona la sciovia?** dä/fē'nō ä ke ō'rä fōōntsyō'nä lä shēōvē'ä?
Has the cross-country skiing track been laid down?	**La pista di fondo è tracciata?** lä pē'stä dē fōn'dō e trätshä'tä?

Skiing

avalanche warning	**il pericolo di valanghe** ēl perē'kōlō dē välän'ge
binding	**l'attacco** lätä'kō
chair lift	**la seggiovia** lä sejovē'ä
cross-country skiing	**lo sci di fondo** lō shē dē fōn'dō
cross-country track	**la pista di fondo** lä pē'stä dē fōn'dō
downhill run	**la discesa** lä dēshe'sä
ice	**il ghiaccio** ēl gyä'tshō
– skating	**pattinare** pätēnä're
icy	**ghiacciato** gyätshä'tō
lift pass	**lo ski-pass** lō skē'päs
children's –	**lo ski-pass per bambini** lō skē'päs per bämbē'nē
half-day –	**lo ski-pass per mezza giornata** lō skē'päs per me'tsä jōrnä'tä
week –	**lo ski-pass settimanale** lō skē'päs setēmänä'le
piste	**la pista** lä pē'stä
black –	**la pista nera** lä pē'stä ne'rä
blue –	**la pista blu** lä pē'stä blōō
red –	**la pista rossa** lä pē'stä rō'ssä

183

poma lift	**la sciovia** lä shēōvē'ä
ski lift	**la sciovia** lä shēōvē'ä
ski poles	**i bastoncini** ē bästōntshē'nē
ski wax	**la sciolina** lä shēōlē'nä
skiing	**lo sci** lō shē
– goggles	**gli occhiali da sci** lyē ōkyä'lē dä shē
– instructor	**il maestro di sci** ēl mä·es'trō dē shē
– lessons	**il corso di sci** ēl kōr'sō dē shē
snow	**la neve** lä ne've
to go tobogganing	**andare in slitta** ändä're ēn slē'tä
toboggan course	**la pista per slitte** lä pē'stä per slē'te
tow lift	**lo ski-lift** lō skē'lēft

MORE SPORTS AND GAMES

Do you have any *playing cards/ board games*?	**Ha *delle carte da gioco/dei giochi di società*?** ä de'le kär'te dä jō'kō/de'ē jō'kē dē sōtshetä'?
What sports do you participate in?	**Che sport pratica Lei?** ke spôrt prä'tēkä le'ē?
Do you play chess?	**Gioca a scacchi?** jō'kä ä skä'kē?
I'd like to take a … course.	**Vorrei fare un corso di …** vōre'ē fä're ōōn kōr'sō dē …
May I join in?	**Posso giocare anch'io?** pô'sō jōkä're änkē'ō?

184

| We'd like to rent a *tennis/squash* court for *an hour/half an hour*. | **Vorremmo avere un campo da *tennis/squash* per *un'ora/mezz'ora*.** vōre'mō äve're ōōn käm'pō dä *te'nēs/skōō-ōsh'* per *ōōnō'rä/metsō'rä*. |
| I'd like to rent ... | **Vorrei noleggiare ...** vōre'ē nōlejä're ... |

Sports and Games

athletic	**sportivo** spōrtē'vō
badminton	**il badminton** ēl bed'mēntōn
bait	**l'esca** le'skä
ball	**la palla** lä pä'lä
basketball	**la pallacanestro** lä päläkänes'trō
beginner *(female)*	**la principiante** lä prēntshēpyän'te
beginner *(male)*	**il principiante** ēl prēntshēpyän'te
bicycle	**la bicicletta** lä bētshēkle'tä
bike hike	**il giro in bicicletta** ēl jē'rō ēn bētshēkle'tä
bowling	**il bowling** ēl bōō'lēng
canoe	**la canoa** lä känō'ä
card game	**la partita a carte** lä pärte'tä ä kär'te
changing rooms	**gli spogliatoi** lyē spōlyätoi'
coach	**l'allenatore** lälenätō're
competition	**la gara** lä gä'rä
course	**il corso** ēl kōr'sō
to cycle, to go cycling	**andare in bicicletta** ändä're ēn bētshēkle'tä
finishing line	**il traguardo** ēl trägōō-är'dō
first half *(of a game)*	**il primo tempo** ēl prē'mō tem'pō

185

to go fishing	**andare a pesca** ändä′re ä pes′kä
fishing license	**la licenza di pesca** lä lētshen′tsä dē pe′skä
fishing rod	**la canna da pesca** lä kä′nä dä pe′skä
game	**la partita** lä pärtē′tä
goal	**il goal** ēl gōl
– keeper	**il portiere** ēl pōrtye′re
golf	**il golf** ēl gōlf
– club	**la mazza da golf** lä mä′tsä dä gōlf
– course	**il campo da golf** ēl käm′pō dä gōlf
gymnastics	**la ginnastica** lä jēnä′stēkä
handball	**la palla a mano** lä pä′lä ä mä′nō
hang-gliding	**lo sport del deltaplano** lō spôrt del deltäplä′nō
horse	**il cavallo** ēl kävä′lō
jazz dancing	**la danza jazz** lä dän′tsä jets
to jog	**fare jogging** fä′re jō′gēng
kayak	**il kayak** ēl käyäk′
to lose	**perdere** per′dere
mini-golf course	**la pista di minigolf** lä pē′stä dē mēnēgōlf′
paragliding	**il parapendio** ēl päräpendē′ō
to play	**giocare** jōkä′re
to go rafting	**il rafting** ēl räf′tēn
referee	**l'arbitro** lär′bētrō
regatta	**la regata** lä regä′tä
to ride a horse	**cavalcare** kävälkä′re
second half	**il secondo tempo** ēl sekōn′dō tem′pō
(of a game)	

186

skydiving	**il paracadutismo** ēl päräkädōōtēz'mō
soccer	**il calcio** ēl käl'tshō
– field	**il campo di calcio** ēl käm'pō dē käl'tshō
– game	**la partita di calcio** lä pärtē'tä dē käl'tshō
sports	**lo sport** lō spōrt
– studio	**la palestra** lä päles'trä
– field	**il campo sportivo** ēl käm'pō spōrtē'vō
squash	**lo squash** lō skōō-ōsh'
– ball	**la palla da squash** lä pä'lä dä skōō-ōsh'
– court	**il campo da squash** ēl käm'pō dä skōō-ōsh'
– raquet	**la racchetta da squash** lä räke'tä dä skōō-ōsh'
start	**la partenza** lä pärten'tsä
table tennis	**il ping-pong** ēl pēng-pōng'
team	**la squadra** lä skōō-ä'drä
tennis	**il tennis** ēl te'nēs
– ball	**la palla da tennis** lä pä'lä dä te'nēs
– court	**il campo da tennis** ēl käm'pō dä te'nēs
– racket	**la racchetta da tennis** lä räke'tä dä te'nēs
victory	**la vittoria** lä vētōr'yä
volleyball	**la pallavolo** lä pälävō'lō
to win	**vincere** vēn'tshere

7

187

CULTURE AND FESTIVALS

At the Box Office

centro tshen'trō	middle
destra des'trä	right
Entrata enträ'tä	entrance
eusaurito esourē'tō	sold out
Fila fē'lä	row
Galleria gälerē'ä	level
Palco päl'kō	box
Platea pläte'ä	orchestra
Posto pō'stō	seat
sinistra sēnēs'trä	left
Uscita di sicurezza	emergency exit
ōōshē'tä dē sēkōōre'tsä	

INFO In the summer, there are theatrical performances and concerts in ancient amphitheaters; for example, in Taormina or Verona. Almost every village or town holds a **sagra** (folk festival) in which food typical of the region is celebrated; for example in the **sagra del gambero** sä'grä del gäm'berō (festival of prawns). The event often starts off with a parade and ends with fireworks (**fuochi d'artificio** fōō-ō'kē därtēfē'tshō).

In many towns there are also traditional festivals, during which actors wear historical costumes; for example in the **calcio storico fiorentino** käl'tshō stō'rēkō fyōrentē'no (medieval soccer game) in Florence, or in the **corsa dei ceri** kōr'sä de'ē tshe'rē (a race with giant candles) in Gubbio.

188

Do you have a schedule of events?	**Ha un programma delle manifesta- zioni?** ä ōōn prōgrä'mä de'le mänēfestätsyō'nē?
Where can I get tickets?	**Dove si comprano i biglietti?** dō've sē kōm'pränō ē bēlye'tē?
When does the *performance/concert* start?	**A che ora inizia lo spettacolo/il con- certo?** ä ke ō'rä ēnē'tsyä lō spetä'kōlō/ēl kōntsher'tō?
When is general admission?	**Da che ora si può entrare?** dä ke ō'rä sē pōō·ō' enträ're?
Are the seats numbered?	**I posti sono numerati?** ē pō'stē sō'nō nōōmerä'tē?
Can I reserve tickets?	**Si possono riservare dei biglietti?** sē pō'sōnō rēservä're de'ē bēlye'tē?
Do you still have tickets for *today/ tomorrow*?	**Ci sono ancora dei biglietti per *oggi/ domani*?** tshē sō'nō änkō'rä de'ē bēlye'tē per ō'jē/dōmä'nē?
How much is a ticket?	**Quanto costa il biglietto?** kōō·än'tō kō'stä ēl bēlye'tō?
Is there a discount for ...	**C'è una riduzione per ...** tshe ōō'nä rēdōōtsyō'ne per ...
children?	**bambini?** bämbē'nē?
senior citizens?	**gli anziani?** lyē äntsyä'nē?
students?	**gli studenti?** lyē stōōden'tē?

I'd like *one ticket/two tickets* for …	**Un biglietto/Due biglietti** per …, per favore. ōōn bēlye'tō/dōō'e bēlye'tē per …, per fävo're.
today.	**oggi** ō'jē
this evening.	**stasera** stäse'rä
the matinee.	**la matinée** lä mätēne'
tomorrow.	**domani** dōmä'nē
the day after tomorrow.	**dopodomani** dōpodōmä'nē
When is the performance over?	**A che ora finisce lo spettacolo?** ä ke ō'rä fēnē'she lō spetä'kōlō?
I'd like to rent an opera glass.	**Vorrei prendere in prestito un binocolo da teatro.** vōre'ē pren'dere ēn pre'stētō ōōn bēnō'kōlō dä te-ä'trō.

Culture and Festivals

act	**l'atto** lä'tō
actor	**l'attore** *m* lätō're
actress	**l'attrice** *f* lätrē'tshe
advance booking	**la prevendita** lä preven'dētä
ballet	**il balletto** ēl bäle'tō
beginning	**l'inizio** lēnē'tsyō
box office	**la cassa** lä kä'sä
cabaret	**il cabaret** ēl käbäre'
chamber music	**la musica da camera** lä mōōsēkä dä kä'merä
choir	**il coro** ēl kō'rō

190

circus	**il circo** ēl tshēr'kō
cloakroom	**il guardaroba** ēl gōō-ärdärō'bä
comedy	**la commedia** lä kōme'dyä
composer *(female)*	**la compositrice** lä kōmpōsētrē'tshe
composer *(male)*	**il compositore** ēl kōmpōsētō're
concert	**il concerto** ēl kōntsher'tō
– hall	**la sala da concerti** lä sä'lä dä kōntsher'tē
conductor	**il direttore d'orchestra** ēl dēretō're dōrkes'trä
dancer *(male)*	**il ballerino** ēl bälerē'nō
dancer *(female)*	**la ballerina** lä bälerē'nä
director *(male)*	**il regista** ēl rejē'stä
director *(female)*	**la regista** lä rejē'sta
discount	**la riduzione** lä rēdōōtsyō'ne
dubbed	**doppiato** dōpyä'tō
end	**la fine** lä fē'ne
folklore evening	**la serata folkloristica** lä serä'tä fōlklōrē'stēkä
grand piano	**il pianoforte a coda** ēl pyänōfōr'te ä kō'dä
intermission	**l'intervallo** lēntervä'lō
leading role	**il ruolo principale** ēl rōō-ō'lō prēntshēpä'le
movie	**il film** ēl fēlm
– theater	**il cinema** ēl tshē'nemä
music	**la musica** lä mōō'zēkä
musical *(play)*	**il musical** ēl myōō'zēkōl
open-air theater	**il teatro all'aperto** ēl te-ä'trō äläper'tō

opera	**l'opera** lō'perä
operetta	**l'operetta** lōpere'tä
orchestra	**l'orchestra** lōrkes'trä
to perform	**recitare** retshētä're
performance	**lo spettacolo** lō spetä'kōlō
play	**l'opera teatrale** lō'perä te-äträ'le
to play *(music)*	**suonare** sōō-ōnä're
premiere	**la prima** lä prē'mä
program	**il programma** ēl prōgrä'mä
seat	**il posto** ēl pō'stō
singer *(male)*	**il cantante** ēl käntän'te
singer *(female)*	**la cantante** lä käntän'te
stage	**il palcoscenico** ēl pälkōshe'nēkō
subtitled	**con i sottotitoli** kōn ē sōtōtē'tōlē
theater	**il teatro** ēl te-ä'trō
ticket	**il biglietto (d'ingresso)**
	ēl bēlye'tō (dēngre'sō)
variety show	**il varietà** ēl väryetä'
vocal recital	**la serata liederistica**
	lä serä'tä lēdere'stēkä

GOING OUT IN THE EVENING

| Is there a nice bar around here? | **C'è un locale simpatico da queste parti?** tshe ōōn lōkä'le sēmpä'tēkō dä kōō·e'ste pär'tē? |
| Where can you go dancing around here? | **Dove si può andare a ballare da queste parti?** dō've sē pōō·ō' ändä're ä bälä're dä kōō·e'ste pär'tē? |

May I sit here?	**È libero qui?** e lě'berǒ kōō·ē'?
Can you get something to eat here?	**Si può anche mangiare qualcosa qui?** sē pōō·ō' än'ke mänjä're kōō·älkō'sä kōō·ē'?
Do you have a drinks menu?	**Ha una carta delle bevande?** ä ōō'nä kär'tä de'le bevän'de?

> **!** **Nel biglietto d'ingresso è inclusa una consumazione.** nel bēlye'tō dēngre'sō e ēnklōō'zä ōō'nä kōnzōōmätsyo'ne. — A drink is included in the price of the ticket. **7**

I'd like a *beer/glass of wine*, please.	**Una birra/Un bicchiere di vino**, per favore. ōō'nä bē'rä/ōōn bēkye're dē vē'nō, per fävō're.
The same again, please.	**Un altro, per favore.** ōōn äl'trō, per fävō're.
What would you like to drink?	**Che cosa Le/ti andrebbe di bere?** ke kō'sä *le/tē* ändre'be dē be're?
May I buy you something to drink?	**Le/Ti posso offrire qualcosa da bere?** *le/tē* pō'sō ōfrē're kōō·älkō'sä dä be're?

➥ *see also: Food and Drink (p. 107)*

| Would you like to dance? | **Vuole/Vuoi ballare?** vōō·ōle/vōō·oi' bälä're? |
| You dance very well. | **Balla/Balli molto bene.** bä'lä/bä'lē mōl'tō be'ne. |

Going out in the Evening

bar *(counter)*	**il bar** ēl bär
bistro	**il locale** ēl lōkä'le
casino	**il casinò** ēl käsēnō'
dance	**il ballo** ēl bä'lō
to dance	**ballare** bälä're
disco	**la discoteca** lä dēskōte'kä
to drink	**bere** be're
evening dress	**l'abito da sera** lä'bētō dä se'rä

Post Office and Bank

POST, TELEGRAMS, TELEPHONE

Letters and Parcels

Where is the nearest mailbox?	**Dov'è la cassetta postale più vicina?** dōve′ lä käse′tä pōstä′le pyōō vētshē′nä?
Where is the nearest post office?	**Dov'è l'ufficio postale più vicino?** dōve′ lōōfē′tshō pōstä′le pyōō vētshē′nō?
How much does a *letter/postcard* to the United States cost?	**Quanto costa spedire una *lettera/cartolina* per l'America?** kōō·än′tō kō′stä spedē′re ōō′nä *le′terä/kärtōle′nä* per läme′rēkä?
Five …-lire stamps, please.	**Cinque francobolli da …Lire, per favore.** tshēn′kōō·e fränkōbō′lē dä …lē′re, per fävō′re.
I'd like to mail this *letter/package* …, please.	**Vorrei spedire *questa lettera/questo pacchetto* …** vōre′ē spedē′re *kōō·e′stä le′terä/kōō·e′stō* päke′tō …
by registered mail	**per raccomandata.** per räkōmändä′tä.
by airmail	**per via aerea.** per vē′ä ä·e′re·ä.
by express mail	**per espresso.** per espre′sō.
I'd like to send a package.	**Vorrei spedire un pacco.** vōre′ē spedē′re ōōn pä′kō.
Where is the general-delivery counter?	**Dov'è lo sportello del fermo posta?** dōve′ lō spōrte′lō del fer′mō pō′stä?

196

| Is there any mail for me? | **C'è posta per me?** tshe pōˈstä per me? |

The Line Home

Can I send a telegram from here?	**Vorrei mandare un telegramma. Posso farlo qui?** vōreˈē mändäˈre ōōn telegräˈmä. pōˈsō färˈlō kōō-ēˈ?
Please give me a form for a telegram.	**Un modulo per telegrammi, per favore.** ōōn mōˈdōōlō per telegräˈmē, per fävōˈre.
Where can I make a phone call?	**Dov'è che si può telefonare qui?** dōveˈ ke sē pōō-ōˈ telefōnäˈre kōō-ēˈ?

INFO In Italy you will find telephones at post offices, bars, and tobacconist's. These will be marked by a yellow sign with a phone receiver. Most telephones use either cards or coins; recently phones have been installed that only use telephone cards. You can get a telephone card (**carta telefonica** kärˈtä telefōˈnēkä) at the post office and tobacconist's. Before you can use it, you must break off (**strappare** sträpäˈre) one corner of the card.

| Could you tell me where I might find a phone booth? | **Mi saprebbe dire per favore dov'è una cabina telefonica?** mē säpreˈbe dēˈre per fävōˈre dōveˈ ōōˈnä käbēˈnä telefōˈnēkä? |

! **Vada alla cabina ...**   Go into booth ...
• väˈdä äˈlä käbēˈnä ...

197

Where can I get a telephone card?	**Dove posso comprare una carta telefonica?** dō've pō'sō kömprä're ōō'nä kär'tä telefō'nēkä?
Could you give me some change for this bill?	**Mi potrebbe cambiare questa banco-nota?** mē pōtre'be kämbyä're kōō·e'stä bänkönō'tä?
What's the area code for ...?	**Qual è il prefisso di ...?** kōō·äl' e ēl prefe'sō dē ...?

INFO   In order to phone someone in the United States, first dial 001 (international code + code for the US and Canada), then the area code (without any further prefix), and then the telephone number.

! **La linea è** *occupata/disturbata.* lä lē'ne·ä e *ōkōōpä'tä/dēstōōrbä'tä.*	The line is *busy/out of order.*
! **Non risponde nessuno.** nōn rēspōn'de nesōō'nō.	There's no answer.
! **Provi ancora una volta.** prō've änkō'rä ōō'nä vōl'tä.	You'll have to try again.

When do evening rates apply?	**Da che ora è valida la tariffa notturna?** dä ke ō'rä e vä'lēdä lä tärē'fä nōtōōr'nä?
I'd like to place a call to the United States.	**Vorrei fare una telefonata in America.** vōre'ē fä're ōō'nä telefōnä'tä ēn äme'rēkä.

addressee	**il destinatario** ēl destēnätär'yō
area code	**il prefisso** ēl prefē'sō
busy	**occupato** ōkōōpä'tō
by airmail	**via aerea** vē'ä ä·e're·ä
charge	**la tariffa** lä tärē'fä
COD	**il contrassegno** ēl kōnträsen'yō
collect call	**la telefonata a carico del ricevente** lä telefōnä'tä ä kä'rēkō del rētsheven'te
to connect *(a call)*	**passare** päsä're
counter	**lo sportello** lō spōrte'lō
envelope	**la busta** lä bōō'stä
express letter	**l'espresso** lespre'sō
fax	**il telefax** ēl te'lefäks
international call	**la telefonata internazionale** lä telefōnä'tä ēnternätsyōnä'le
letter	**la lettera** lä le'terä
mailbox	**la cassetta delle lettere** lä käse'tä de'le le'tere
package	**il pacco** ēl pä'kō
– info form	**il bollettino di spedizione dei pacchi postali** ēl bōletē'nō dē spedētsyō'ne de'ē pä'kē pōstä'lē
parcel	**il pacchetto** ēl päke'tō
pay phone	**il telefono a monete** ēl tele'fōnō ä mōne'te
phone that operates with a phone card	**il telefono a schede** ēl tele'fōnō ä ske'de

8

199

post office	**la posta** lä pō'stä
postcard	**la cartolina (illustrata)**
	lä kärtōlē'nä (ēlōōsträ'tä)
to send	**spedire** spedē're
stamp	**il francobollo** ēl fränkōbō'lō
– vending machine	**il distributore automatico di francobolli** ēl dēstrēbōōtō're outōmä'tēkō dē fränkōbō'lē
telegram	**il telegramma** ēl telegrä'mä
telephone	**il telefono** ēl tele'fōnō
– booth	**la cabina telefonica**
	lä käbē'nä telefō'nēkä
– card	**la carta telefonica**
	lä kär'tä telefō'nēkä
– conversation	**la telefonata** lä telefōnä'tä
– directory	**l'elenco telefonico**
	lelen'kō telefō'nēkō
– number	**il numero di telefono**
	ēl nōō'merō dē telefō'nō
to make a telephone call	**telefonare** telefōnä're
ZIP code	**il codice di avviamento postale** ēl kō'dētshe dē ävyämen'tō pōstä'le

MONEY MATTERS

Can you tell me where I can find a bank around here?	**Scusi, c´è una banca qui vicino?** skōō'zē, tshe ōō'nä bän'kä kōō·e' vētshē'nō?
Where can I exchange foreign currency?	**Dove posso cambiare dei soldi?** dō've pō'sō kämbyä're de'ē sōl'dē?
What's the commission charge?	**A quanto ammontano le spese bancarie?** ä kōō·än'tō ämōn'tänō le spe'se bänkär'ye?
What time does the bank close?	**Fino a che ora è aperta la banca?** fē'nō ä ke ō'rä e äper'tä lä bän'kä?

8

INFO Banks are open from Monday to Friday in the morning until 1 p.m., and then again in the afternoon for only one hour. You can also exchange money at an **agenzia di cambio** äjen'tsyä dē käm'byō. It has longer opening hours than a bank, but it has also a less advantageous exchange rate.

I'd like to change … dollars into lire.	**Vorrei cambiare … dollari in Lire.** vōre'ē kämbyä're … dōl'ärē ēn lē're.
Someone is wiring me money. Has it arrived yet?	**Mi sono fatto mandare un vaglia telegrafico. È già arrivato?** mē sō'nō fä'tō mändä're ōōn vä'lyä telegrä'fēkō. e jä ärēvä'tō?

201

| Can I use my credit card to get cash? | **Posso avere del denaro in contanti con la mia carta di credito?** pō'sō äve're del denä'rō ēn kōntän'tē kōn lä mē'ä kär'tä dē kre'dētō? |
| I'd like to cash a traveler's check. | **Vorrei riscuotere un traveller's cheque.** vōre'ē rēskōō·ōte're ōōn trä'velers·shek. |

! Il Suo passaporto/La Sua carta d'identità, per favore. el sōō'ō päsäpōr'tō/lä sōō'ä kär'tä dēdentētä', per fävō're.	May I see your *passport/ID*, please?
! Firmi qui, per favore. fēr'mē kōō·ē', per fävō're.	Would you sign here, please?
! Per ritirare il denaro si accomodi alla cassa. per rētērä're el denä'rō sē äkō'mōdē ä'lä kä'sä.	You can pick up the money at the cashier.
? Che tagli preferisce? ke tä'lyē frefe'rē'she?	How would you like the money?

| In small bills, please. | **Banconote di piccolo taglio, per favore.** bänkōnō'te dē pē'kōlō tä'lyō, per fävō're. |
| Please give me some change, too. | **Mi dia anche un po' di spiccioli, per favore.** mē dē'ä än'ke ōōn pō dē spē'tshōlē, per fävō're. |

ATM	**la cassa automatica prelievi**
	lä kä'sä outōmä''tēkä prelye'vē
bank	**la banca** lä bän'kä
– account	**il conto in banca**
	ēl kōn'tō ēn bän'kä
– code	**il codice di avviamento bancario**
	ēl kōdētshe bänkärēō bänkär'yō
– transfer	**il bonifico (bancario)**
	ēl bōnēfēkō (bänkär'yō)
bill	**la banconota** lä bänkōnō'tä
card number	**il numero della carta assegni**
	ēl nōō'merō de'lä kär'tä äse'nyē
cash	**il denaro in contanti**
	ēl denä'rō ēn kōntän'tē
cashier	**la cassa** lä kä'sä
change	**gli spiccioli** lyē spē'tshōlē
check	**l'assegno** läse'nyō
check card	**la carta assegni** lä kär'tä äse'nyē
PIN	**il numero segreto**
	ēl nōō'mero segre'tō
commission	**la tariffa** lä tärē'fä
counter	**lo sportello** lō spōrte'lō
credit card	**la carta di credito** lä kär'tä dē kredē'tō
currency exchange	**l'agenzia di cambio**
	läjen'tsyä dē käm'byō
dollar	**il dollaro** ēl dō'lärō
to exchange	**cambiare** kämbyä're
exchange rate	**il cambio** ēl käm'byō

8

203

money	**il denaro, i soldi** ēl denä'rō, ē sōl'dē	
savings account	**il libretto di risparmio**	
	ēl lēbre'tō dē rēspär'myō	
savings bank	**la cassa di risparmio**	
	lä kä'sä dē rēspär'myō	
signature	**la firma** lä fēr'mä	
total amount	**l'importo** lēmpōr'tō	
traveler's check	**il traveller's cheque** ēl tre'velers·shek	
to withdraw	**prelevare** prelevä're	

Emergencies

HEALTH

Information

Could you recommend a general practitioner?	**Mi può consigliare un medico generico?** mē pōō-ò kōnsēlyä're ōōn me'dēkō jene'rēkō?
Does *he/she* speak English?	**Parla inglese?** pär'lä ēn-gle'se?
What are *his/her* office hours?	**Quando riceve?** kōō-än'dō rētshe've?
Where is *his/her* practice?	**Dov'è il suo ambulatorio?** dōve' ēl sōō'ō ämbōōlätōr'yō?

INFO If there is an accident, you must contact the **pronto soccorso** prōn'tō sōkōr'sō (first aid) of the nearest hospital, and they will pick up the injured person in an ambulance. If someone is seriously ill, get in touch with the **guardia medica** gōō-är'dyä me'dēkä, the local doctor on call for emergencies, who will visit the patient at home. If you don't know what to do, the **carabinieri** käräbēnye're̅ (police) will help you; they can be reached at telephone number 113 anywhere in Italy.

Can *he/she* make house calls?	**Fa visite a domicilio?** fä vēze'tē ä dōmētshē'lyō?
My *husband/wife* is sick.	*Mio marito/Mia moglie* **sta male.** mē'ō märē'tō/mē'ä mō'lye stä mä'le.

206

| Please call *an ambulance/the emergency doctor*! | **Chiami *un'ambulanza/la guardia medica*!** kyä'mē ōōnämbōōlän'tsä/lä gōō·är'dyä me'dēkä! |

| Where are you taking *him/her*? | **Dove *lo/la* portate?** dō've *lō/lä* pōrtä'te? |

| I'd like to come with you. | **Vorrei venire anch'io.** vōre'ē venē're änke'ō. |

| Where's the nearest (24-hour) pharmacy? | **Dov'è la farmacia (con servizio notturno) più vicina?** dōve' lä färmätshē'ä (kōn serve'tsyō nōtōōr'nō) pyōō vētshē'nä? |

Drugstore

| Do you have anything for ...? | **Ha qualcosa contro ...?** ä kōō·älkō'sä kōn'trō ...? |

➡ *Diseases, Doctor, Hospital (p. 219)*

| *How/When* should I take it? | ***Come/Quando* la devo prendere?** *kō'me/kōō·än'dō* lä de'vō pren'dere? |

| I need this medicine. | **Mi serve questa medicina.** mē ser've kōō·e'stä medētshē'nä. |

| ❗ **Per questa medicina ci vuole la ricetta.** per kōō·e'stä medētshē'nä tshē vōō·ō'le lä rētshe'tä. | You need a prescription for this medicine. |

| ❗ **Al momento non l'abbiamo.** äl mōmen'tō nōn läbyä'mō. | I'm sorry, but we don't have that here. |

! **Dobbiamo ordinarlo.**	We'll have to order it.
• dōbyä'mō ōrdēnär'lō.	

When can I pick it up?	**Quando posso averla?**
	kōō·än'dō pō'sō äver'lä?

Patient Package Insert

a digiuno, a stomaco vuoto	on an empty stomach
ä dējōō'nō, ä stō'mäkō vōō-ō'tō	
dopo i pasti dō'pō ē pä'stē	after meals
effetti collaterali efē'tē kōläterä'lē	side effects
far sciogliere in bocca	allow to dissolve on
fär shō'lyere ēn bō'kä	the tongue
per uso esterno per ōō'zō ester'nō	external
per uso interno per ōō'zō enter'nō	internal
per via rettale per vē'ä retä'le	rectally
prima dei pasti prē'mä de'ē pä'stē	before meals
secondo le indicazioni del medico	according to the
sekōn'dō le ēndēkätsyō'nē del me'dēkō	doctor's instructions
senza masticare sen'tsä mästēkä're	swallow whole
tre volte al giorno tre vōl'te äl jōr'nō	three times a day

Drugstore

alcohol	**l'alcool (denaturato)** *m*
	läl'kō-ōl (denätōōrä'tō)
antibiotic	**l'antibiotico** läntēbē-ō'tēkō
antiseptic ointment	**la pomata per le ferite**
	lä pōmä'tä per le ferē'te

Band-Aid®	**il cerotto** ēl tsherō'tō
birth-control pill	**la pillola anticoncezionale** lä pē'lōlä äntēkōntshetsyōnä'le
charcoal tablets	**le compresse al carbone vegetale** le kōmpre'se äl kärbō'ne vejetä'le
circulatory stimulant	**un farmaco contro i disturbi circolatori** ōōn fär'mäkō kōn'trō ē dēstōōr'bē tshērkōlätō'rē
condoms	**i profilattici, i preservativi** ē prōfēlä'tētshē, ē preservätē'vē
cotton	**il cotone idrofilo** ēl kōtō'ne ēdrō'fēlō
cough syrup	**lo sciroppo per la tosse** lō shērō'pō per lä tō'se
disinfectant	**il disinfettante** ēl dēsēnfetän'te
drops	**le gocce** le gō'tshe
elastic bandage	**la benda elastica** lä ben'dä elä'stēkä
fever	**la febbre** lä fe'bre
medicine to reduce –	**l'antipiretico** läntēpēre'tēkō
first-aid kit	**le bende** le ben'de
gauze bandage	**la garza** lä gär'tsä
homeopathic	**omeopatico** ōme·ōpä'tēkō
iodine	**lo iodio** lō yō'dyō
laxative	**il lassativo** ēl lässätē'vō
night duty	**il servizio notturno** ēl servē'tsyō nōtōōr'nō
ointment	**la pomata** lä pōmä'tä
– for mosquito bites	**la pomata contro le punture di zanzare** lä pōmä'tä kōn'trō le pōōntōō're dē dzändzä're

– for sun allergy	**la pomata contro l'eritema solare**
	lä pōmä'tä kōn'trō lerēte'mä sōlä're
painkiller	**l'analgesico** lä'nälje'sēkō
pharmacy	**la farmacia** lä färmätshē'ä
powder	**la polverina** lä pōlverē'nä
prescription	**la ricetta** lä rētshe'tä
sanitary napkins	**gli assorbenti igienici**
	lyē äsōrben'tē ēj·e'nētshē
sleeping pills	**il sonnifero** ēl sōnē'ferō
something for ...	**qualcosa contro ...** kōō·älkō'sä kōn'trō ...
suppository	**la supposta** lä sōōpō'stä
tablet	**la compressa** lä kōmpre'sä
talcum powder	**il borotalco** ēl bōrōtäl'kō
tampons	**i tamponi** ē tämpō'nē
thermometer	**il termometro** ēl termō'metrō
tranquilizer	**il calmante** ēl kälmän'te

➡️ *see also: Diseases, Doctor, Hospital (S. 219)*

At the Doctor's

I have a (bad) cold.	**Ho un (forte) raffreddore.**
	ō ōōn (fōr'te) räfredō're.
I have *diarrhea/* *a (high) fever.*	**Ho la *diarrea/febbre (alta)*.**
	ō lä *dyäre'ä/fe'bre (äl'tä).*
I don't feel well.	**Non mi sento bene.** nōn mē sen'tō be'ne.
I feel nauseous.	**Ho la nausea.** ō lä näōō'seä.
I'm dizzy.	**Mi gira la testa.** mē jē'rä lä te'stä.

Address doctors only by their title of **dottore** dōtō're, or **dotoressa** dōtōre'sä if the doctor is a woman.

My … *hurts/hurt*.	**Mi** *fa/fanno* **male …** mē *fä/fä'nō* mä'le …

➡️ *Parts of the Body and Organs (p. 217)*

I have pains here.	**Ho dei dolori qui.** ō de'ē dōlō'rē kōō·ē'.
I've been vomiting (a lot).	**Ho vomitato (più volte).** ō vōmētä'tō (pyōō vōl'te).
My stomach is upset.	**Ho fatto indigestione.** ō fä'tō ēndējestyō'ne.
I fainted.	**Sono ♂ svenuto/♀ svenuta.** sō'nō ♂ zvenōō'tō/♀ zvenōō'tä.
I can't move …	**Non posso muovere …** nōn pō'sō mōō·ō'vere …

➡️ *Parts of the Body and Organs (p. 217)*

I've hurt myself.	**Mi sono ♂ ferito/♀ ferita.** mē sō'nō ♂ ferē'tō/♀ ferē'tä.
I had a fall.	**Sono ♂ caduto/♀ caduta.** sō'nō ♂ kädōō'tō/♀ kädōō'tä.
I've been *stung/bitten* by …	**Mi ha** *punto/morso* **…** mē ä *pōōn'tō/mōr'sō* …

9

211

I have (not) been vaccinated against …	**(Non) sono** ♂ **vaccinato/** ♀ **vaccinata contro …** (nôn) sō'nō ♂ vätshēnä'tō/ ♀ vätshēnä'tä kōn'trō …
I'm allergic to penicillin.	**Sono** ♂ **allergico/** ♀ **allergica alla penicillina.** sō'nō ♂ äler'jēkō/ ♀ äler'jēkä ä'lä penētshēlē'nä.
I have *high/low* blood pressure.	**Ho la pressione** *alta/bassa.* ō lä presyō'ne *äl'tä/bä'sä.*
I have a pacemaker.	**Ho il pace-maker.** ō ēl pēēs'mekä.
I'm … months pregnant.	**Sono al … mese di gravidanza.** sō'nō äl … me'se dē grävēdän'tsä.
I'm diabetic.	**Sono** ♂ **diabetico/** ♀ **diabetica.** sō'nō ♂ dē-äbe'tēkō/ ♀ dē-äbe'tēkä.
I'm HIV-positive.	**Sono** ♂ **sieropositivo/** ♀ **sieropositiva.** sō'nō ♂ syerōpōsētē'vō ♀ syerōpōsētē'vä.
I take this medicine regularly.	**Prendo regolarmente queste medicine.** pren'dō regōlärmen'te kōō-e'ste medētshē'ne.

Che disturbi ha? ke dēstoōr'bē ä? | What are your symptoms?

Dov'è che le fa male? dōve' ke le fä mä'le? | Where does it hurt?

Le da fastidio? le dä fästë'dyō? | Does that hurt?

Apra la bocca. ä'prä lä bō'kä. | Open your mouth, please.

Mi faccia vedere la lingua. mē fä'tshä vede're lä lēn'gōō·ä. | Show me your tongue, please.

Tossisca. tōsē'skä. | Cough.

Si spogli, per favore. sē spō'lyē, per fävō're. | Would you get undressed, please.

Scopra il braccio, per favore. skō'prä ēl brä'tshō, per fävō're. | Would you roll up your sleeve, please.

Respiri profondamente. Trattenga il respiro. respē'rē prōföndämen'te. träten'gä ēl respē'rō. | Breathe deeply. Now hold your breath.

9

Da quanto tempo ha questi disturbi? dä kōō·än'tō tem'pō ä kōō·e'stē dēstoōr'bē? | How long have you felt this way?

È ♂ vaccinato/♀ vaccinata contro …? e ♂ vätshēnä'tō/♀ vätshēnä'tä kōn'trō …? | Have you been vaccinated against …?

213

Ha un libretto delle vaccinazioni?
ä ōōn lēbre'tō de'le vätshēnatsyō'nē?

Do you have a vaccination record?

Deve fare una radiografia.
de've fä're ōō'nä rädyōgräfē'ä.

We need to take some X-rays.

Si è *♂rotto/♀rotta/♂slogato/♀slo-
gata* ... sē e ♂rō'tō/♀rō'tä/♂zlōgä'tō/
♀zlōgä'tä ...

Your ... is *broken/
sprained.*

Deve fare l'analisi *del sangue/delle
urine.* de've fä're länäl'ēzē *del sän'gōō-e/
de'le ōōrē'ne.*

We need to take a
blood/urine sample.

Deve operarsi. de've ōperär'sē.

You'll have to have
an operation.

Deve andare da uno specialista.
de've ändä're dä ōō'nō spetshälē'stä.

I'll have to refer you
to a specialist.

Non è niente di grave.
nōn e nēen'te dē grä've.

It's nothing serious.

Prenda *... pillole/gocce ...* **volte al
giorno.** pren'dä *... pē'lōle/gō'tshe ...*
vōl'te äl jōr'nō.

Take ... *tablets/drops*
... times a day.

Torni *domani/fra ... giorni.*
tōr'nē *dōmä'nē/frä ... jōr'nē.*

Come back
tomorrow/in ... days.

Is it serious?	**È grave?** e grä've?
Can you give me a doctor's certificate?	**Mi può rilasciare un certificato medico?** mē pōō·ò' rēläshä're ōōn tshertēfēkä'tō me'dēkō?
Do I have to come back again?	**Devo tornare ancora?** de'vō tōrnä're änkō'rä?
What precautions should I take?	**A che cosa devo fare attenzione?** ä ke kō'sä de'vō fä're ätentzyō'ne?
I need a receipt in English for my medical insurance.	**Ho bisogno di una ricevuta (in inglese) per la mia assicurazione.** ō bēzō'nyō dē ōō'nä rētshevōō'tä ēn ēn·gle'se per lä mē'ä äsēkōōrätsyō'ne.

In the Hospital

| Is there anyone here who speaks English? | **C'è qualcuno che parla inglese?** tshe kōō·älkōō'nō ke pär'lä ēn·gle'se? |
| I'd like to speak to a doctor. | **Vorrei parlare con un dottore.** vōre'ē pärlä're kōn ōōn dōtō're. |

➡ *At the Doctor's (p. 210)*

| What's the diagnosis? | **Qual è la diagnosi?** kōō·äl' e lä dē·ä'nyōzē? |

9

215

I'd rather have the operation in the United States.	**Preferirei farmi operare in America.** preferēre'ē fär'mē ōperä're ēn äme'rēkä.
I'm insured for the journey home.	**Sono ♂ assicurato/♀ assicurata per il viaggio di ritorno.** sō'nō ♂ äsēkōōrä'tō/ ♀ äsēkōōrä'tä per ēl vyä'jo dē rētōr'nō.
Would you please notify my family?	**Avvisi la mia famiglia, per favore.** ävē'zē lä mē'ä fämē'lyä, per fävō're.
Can I have a private room?	**Posso avere una camera singola?** pō'sō ave're ōō'nä kä'merä sēn'gōlä?
How long will I have to stay here?	**Per quanto tempo devo rimanere ancora?** per kōō·än'tō tem'pō de'vō rēmäne're änkō'rä?
When can I get out of bed?	**Quando potrò alzarmi?** kōō·än'dō pōtrō' ältsär'mē?
Could you give me something *for the pain/to get to sleep*?	**Mi dia qualcosa *contro i dolori/per dormire*, per favore.** mē dē'ä kōō·älkō'sä *kōn'trō ē dōlō'rē/per dōrmē're*, per fävō're.
I'd like to be discharged. (I'll assume full responsibility.)	**Vorrei essere ♂ dimesso/♀ dimessa (dietro mia responsabilità).** vōre'ē e'sere ♂ dēme'sō/♀ dēme'sä (dye'trō mē'ä respōnsäbēlētä').

Please give me a certificate stating my length of stay here.	**Mi rilasci un certificato con la specificazione della durata della degenza ospedaliera, per favore.** mē rēlä'shē ōōn tshertēfēkä'tō kōn lä spetshēfēkätsyō'ne de'lä dōōrä'tä de'lä dejen'tsä ōspedälye'rä, per fävō're.

Parts of the Body and Organs

abdomen	**l'addome** *m* lädō'me
ankle	**il malleolo** ēl mäle'ōlō
appendix	**l'appendice** *f* läpendē'tshe
arm	**il braccio**, *pl:* **le braccia** ēl brä'tshō, *pl:* le brä'tshä
back	**la schiena** lä skye'nä
bladder	**la vescica** lä veshē'kä
blood	**il sangue** ēl sän'gōō-e
bone	**l'osso** lō'sō
brain	**il cervello** ēl tsherve'lō
bust	**il busto** ēl bōō'stō
calf	**il polpaccio** ēl polpä'tshō
cheek	**la guancia** lä gōō-än'tshä
chest	**il petto** ēl pe'tō
collarbone	**la clavicola** lä klävē'kōlä
disk	**il disco intervertebrale** ēl dē'sko ēntervertebrä'le
ear	**l'orecchio** lōre'kyō
–drum	**la membrana del timpano** lä membrä'nä del tēm'pänō
eye	**l'occhio** lō'kyō

face	**la faccia** lä fä'tshä
finger	**il dito,** *pl:* **le dita** ēl dē'tō, *pl:* le dē'tä
foot	**il piede** ēl pye'de
forehead	**la fronte** lä frōn'te
gall bladder	**la bile** lä bē'le
genitals	**gli organi genitali** lyē ōr'gänē jenētä'lē
gland	**la ghiandola** lä gyän'dōlä
hand	**la mano** lä mä'nō
head	**la testa** lä te'stä
heart	**il cuore** ēl kōō-ō're
hip	**l'anca** län'kä
intestine	**l'intestino** lēntestē'nō
joint	**l'articolazione** *f* lärtēkōlätsyō'ne
kidney	**il rene** ēl re'ne
knee	**il ginocchio** ēl jēnō'kyō
–cap	**la rotula** lä rō'tōōlä
leg	**la gamba** lä gäm'bä
lung	**il polmone** ēl pōlmō'ne
mouth	**la bocca** lä bō'kä
muscle	**il muscolo** ēl mōō'skōlō
neck *(in general)*	**il collo** ēl kō'lō
neck *(nape)*	**la nuca** lä nōō'kä
nerve	**il nervo** ēl ner'vō
nose	**il naso** ēl nä'sō
pelvis	**il bacino** ēl bätshē'nō
penis	**il pene** ēl pe'ne
rib	**la costola** lä kō'stōlä
–cage	**il torace** ēl tōrä'tshe
shin	**la tibia** lä tē'byä

shoulder	la spalla lä spä'lä
– blade	la scapola lä skä'pōlä
sinus	il seno frontale ēl se'nō frŏntä'le
skin	la pelle lä pe'le
spine	la spina dorsale lä spē'nä dōrsä'le
stomach	lo stomaco lō stō'mäkō
tendon	il tendine ēl ten'dēne
thigh	la coscia lä kō'shä
throat	la gola lä gō'lä
thyroid (gland)	la tiroide lä tēroē'de
toe	il dito del piede ēl dē'tō del pye'de
tongue	la lingua lä lēn'gōō·ä
tonsils	le tonsille le tōnsē'le
tooth	il dente ēl den'te
vagina	la vagina lä väje'nä
vein	la vena lä ve'nä
vertebra	la vertebra lä ver'tebrä

Diseases, Doctor, Hospital

abscess	l'ascesso läshe'sō
Aids	l'Aids *m* lääds
allergy	l'allergia lälerjē'ä
appendicitis	l'appendicite *f* läpendētshē'te
asthma	l'asma läz'mä
bite	il morso ēl mōr'sō
blister	la vescica lä veshē'kä
blood	il sangue ēl sän'gōō·e
blood poisoning	la setticemia lä setētshemē'ä

blood pressure	**la pressione (sanguigna)**
	lä presyō'ne (sän-gōō-ē'nyä)
high –	**la pressione alta**
	lä presyō'ne äl'tä
low –	**la pressione bassa** lä presyō'ne bä'sä
blood transfusion	**la trasfusione (del sangue)**
	lä träsfōōzyō'ne (del sän'gōō-e)
blood type	**il gruppo sanguigno**
	ēl grōō'po sän-gōō-ē'nyō
broken	**rotto** rō'tō
bruise	**la contusione** lä kōntōōzyō'ne
burn	**l'ustione** f lōōstyō'ne
cardiac arrest	**l'infarto** lēnfär'tō
certificate	**il certificato** ēl tshertēfēkä'tō
chicken pox	**la varicella** lä värētshe'lä
circulation	**i disturbi circolatori**
problems	ē dēstōōr'bē tshērkōlätō'rē
cold	**il raffreddore** ēl räfredō're
colic	**la colica** lä kō'lēkä
concussion	**la commozione cerebrale**
	lä kōmōtsyō'ne tsherebrä'le
conjunctivitis	**la congiuntivite** lä kōnjōōntēvē'te
cough	**la tosse** lä to'se
cramp	**il crampo** ēl kräm'pō
cystitis	**la cistite** lä tshēstē'te
dermatologist	**il dermatologo** ēl dermätō'lōgō
diabetes	**il diabete** ēl dyäbe'te
diarrhea	**la diarrea** lä dyärē'ä
dislocated	**lussato** lōōsä'tō

220

dizziness	**le vertigini** le verte'jēnē	
doctor *(male)*	**il dottore, il medico**	
	ēl dōtō're, ēl me'dēkō	
doctor *(female)*	**la dottoressa** lä dōtore'sä	
ear infection	**l'otite *f* media** lōtē'te me'dyä	
ear, nose and throat doctor	**l'otorinolaringoiatra**	
	lōtōrēnōlärēn·gōyä'trä	
faint *(feeling)*	**svenuto** zvenōō'tō	
feces	**le feci** le fe'tshē	
fever	**la febbre** lä fe'bre	
flu	**l'influenza** lēnflōō·en'tsä	
food poisoning	**l'intossicazione *f* da alimenti**	
	lēntōsēkätsyō'ne dä älēmen'tē	
fungal infection	**la micosi** lä mēkō'sē	
gallstones	**i calcoli biliari** ē käl'kōlē bēlēä'rē	
general practitioner	**il medico generico** ēl me'dēkō jene'rēkō	
German measles	**la rosolia** lä rōzōlē'ä	
gynecologist *(female)*	**la ginecologa** lä jēnekō'lōgä	
gynecologist *(male)*	**il ginecologo** ēl jēnekō'lōgō	
hay fever	**il raffreddore da fieno**	
	ēl räfredō're dä fye'nō	
headache	**il mal di testa** ēl mäl dē te'stä	
heart	**il cuore** ēl kōō·ō're	
– attack	**l'attacco cardiaco** lätä'kō kärdē'äkō	
– burn	**i bruciori di stomaco**	
	ē brōōtshō're dē stō'mäkō	

– defect	**il difetto cardiaco** ēl dēfe'tō kärdē'äkō
hemorrhage	**l'emorragia** le mōräjē'ä
hernia	**l'ernia inguinale** ler'nē-ä ēngōō-ēnä'le
herpes	**l'herpes** *m* ler'pes
illness	**la malattia** lä mälätē'ä
infection	**l'infezione** *f* lēnfetsyō'ne
infectious	**contagioso** kōntäjō'sō
inflammation	**l'infiammazione** *f* lēnfyämätsyō'ne
injury	**la ferita** lä ferē'tä
internist	**l'internista** *m, f* lēnternē'stä
kidney stones	**i calcoli renali** ē käl'kōlē renä'lē
lumbago	**la lombaggine** lä lōmbä'jēne
measles	**il morbillo** ēl mōrbē'lō
migraine	**l'emicrania** lemēkrä'nēä
mumps	**gli orecchioni** *m/pl* lyē ōrekyō'nē
nausea	**la nausea** lä nou'ze-ä
nose bleed	**l'emorragia nasale** lemōräjē'ä näsä'le
nurse	**l'infermiera** lēnfermye'rä
to operate	**operare** ōperä're
ophthalmologist	**l'oculista** *m* lōkōōlē'stä
orthopedist	**l'ortopedico** lōrtōpe'dēkō
pain(s)	**i dolori** *m/pl* ē dōlō'rē
pediatrician	**il pediatra** ēl pedyä'trä
pneumonia	**la polmonite** lä pōlmōnē'te
poisoning	**l'avvelenamento** lävelenämen'tō
polio	**la poliomielite** lä pōlē-ōmē-elē'te
pregnant	**incinta** ēntshēn'tä
pulled muscle	**lo stiramento** lō stērämen'tō

pulled tendon	**lo stiramento (dei tendini)**
	lō stērämen'tō (de'ē ten'dēnē)
pus	**il pus** ēl pōōs
rash	**l'esantema** *m* lesänte'mä
respiratory problems	**le difficoltà respiratorie**
	le dēfēkōltä' respērätōr'ye
rheumatism	**i reumatismi** *m/pl* ē re-ōōmätēz'mē
scarlet fever	**la scarlattina** lä skärlätē'nä
sciatica	**la sciatica** lä shä'tēka
seasickness	**il mal di mare** ēl mäl dē mä're
the shivers	**i brividi (di febbre)** ē brē'vēdē (dē fe'bre)
shock	**lo shock** lō shōk
sinus infection	**la sinusite** lä sēnōōzē'te
sore throat	**il mal di gola** ēl mäl dē gō'lä
sprained	**slogato** zlōgä'tō
sting	**la puntura** lä pōōntōō'rä
stomachache	**il mal di stomaco** ēl mäl dē stō'mäkō
stomach ulcer	**l'ulcera gastrica** lōōl'tsherä gä'strēkä
stroke	**il colpo apoplettico** ēl kōl'pō äpōple'tēkō
sunstroke	**l'insolazione** *f* lēnsōlätsyō'ne
sunburn	**la scottatura (da sole)**
	lä skōtätōō'rä (dä sō'le)
sweating	**la forte traspirazione**
	lä fōr'te träspērätsyō'ne
swelling	**il gonfiore** ēl gōnfyō're
tetanus	**il tetano** ēl te'tänō
tonsillitis	**la tonsillite** lä tōnsēlē'te
torn ligament	**lo strappo ai legamenti**
	lō strä'pō ī legämen'te

9

ulcer	**l'ulcera** lōōl'tsherä
urine sample	**l'analisi** f **delle urine**
	länä'lēsē de'le ōōrē'ne
urologist	**l'urologo** lōōrō'lōgō
vaccination	**la vaccinazione** lä vätshēnätsyō'ne
– record	**il libretto delle vaccinazioni**
	ēl lēbre'tō de'le vätshēnätsyō'nē
venereal disease	**la malattia venerea** lä mälätē'ä vene're·ä
veterinarian	**il veterinario** ēl veterēnär'yō
vomiting	**il vomito** ēl vō'mētō
ward	**il reparto** ēl repär'tō
whooping cough	**la pertosse** lä pertō'se
wound	**la ferita** lä ferē'tä
to X-ray	**fare una radiografia**
	fä're ōō'nä rädyōgräfē'ä

At the Dentist's

… hurts.	**Mi fa male …** mē fä mä'le …
This tooth here	**questo dente.** kōō·e'stō den'te.
This tooth at the top	**il dente qui sopra.**
	ēl den'te kōō·ē' sō'prä.
This tooth at the bottom	**il dente qui sotto.**
	ēl den'te kōō·ē' sō'tō.
This tooth on the right	**il dente qui a destra.**
	ēl den'te kōō·ē' ä des'trä.
This tooth on the left	**il dente qui a sinistra.**
	ēl den'te kōō·ē' ä sēnēs'trä.

This tooth is broken.	**Mi si è rotto questo dente.** mē sē e rō'tō kōō·e'stō den'te.
I've lost a filling.	**È andata via l'otturazione.** e ändä'tä vē'ä lōtōōrätsyō'ne.
Can you do a temporary job on the tooth?	**Può fare soltanto un trattamento provvisorio?** pōō·ō' fä're sõltän'tō ōōn trätämen'tō prōvēzōr'yō?
Please don't pull the tooth.	**Non mi tolga il dente, per favore.** nōn mē tōl'gä ēl den'te, per fävō're.
Would you give me/I'd rather not have an injection, please.	***Mi faccia/Non mi faccia la puntura.*** mē fä'tshä/nōn mē fä'tshä lä pōōntōō'rä.

What the dentist says

Occorre ... ōkō're ...

    un ponte. ōōn pōn'te.
    un'otturazione. ōōnōtōōrätsyō'ne.
    una corona. ōō'nä kōrō'nä.

You need a ...
    bridge.
    filling.
    crown.

Devo estrarre il dente.
de'vō esträ're ēl den'te.

I'll have to pull the tooth.

Si sciacqui bene la bocca.
sē shä'kōō·ē·be'ne lä bō'kä.

Rinse out your mouth, please.

Non mangi niente per due ore.
nōn män'jē nēen'te per dōō'e ō're.

Don't eat anything for two hours.

9

(local) anesthetic	**l'anestesia (locale)**	länesteze͞'ä (lōkä'le)
braces	**l'apparecchio per i denti**	
	läpäre'kyō per ē den'tē	
bridge	**il ponte**	ēl pōn'te
cavity	**la carie**	lä kär'ye
collar of the tooth	**il collo del dente**	ēl kō'lō del den'te
crown	**la corona**	lä kōrō'nä
gold –	**la corona d'oro**	lä kōrō'nä dō'rō
porcelain –	**la corona di porcellana**	
	lä kōrō'nä dē pōrtshelä'nä	
dentist	**il dentista**	ēl dente̅'stä
dentures	**la dentiera, la protesi**	
	lä dentye'rä, lä prōte'zē	
eye tooth	**il (dente) canino**	ēl (den'te) käne̅'nō
filling	**l'otturazione** *f*	lōtōōrätsyō'ne
amalgam –	**l'otturazione** *f* **di amalgama**	
	lōtōōrätsyō'ne dē ämäl'gämä	
synthetic –	**l'otturazione di materiale sintetico**	
	lōtōōrätsyō'ne dē mäteryä'le	
	sēnte'tēkō	
gums	**la gengiva**	lä jenjē'vä
gum disease	**la paradentosi**	lä päradentō'zē
imprint	**il calco**	ēl käl'kō
incisor	**il dente incisivo**	ēl den'te ēntshēze̅'vō
inflammation	**l'infiammazione** *f*	lēnfyämätsyō'ne
injection	**la puntura**	lä pōōntōō'rä
inlay	**l'otturazione d'oro**	lōtōōrätsyō'ne dō'rō
jaw	**la mascella**	lä mäshe'lä

molar	**il (dente) molare** ēl (den'te) mōlä're
nerve	**il nervo** ēl ner'vō
office hours	**l'orario delle visite** lōrär'yō de'le vē'zēte
orthodontal clinic	**la clinica odontoiatrica** lä klē'nēkä ōdōntōyä'trēkä
pivot tooth	**il dente a perno** ēl den'te ä per'nō
to pull	**estrarre** esträ're
root	**la radice** lä rädē'tshe
– canal work	**il trattamento della radice** ēl trätämen'tō de'lä rädē'tshe
tooth	**il dente** ēl den'te
– decay	**la carie** lä kär'ye
wisdom tooth	**il dente del giudizio** ēl den'te del jōōdē'tsyō

POLICE; LOST AND FOUND

Where is the nearest police station?	**Dov'è il posto di polizia più vicino?** dōve' ēl pō'stō dē pōlētsē'ä pyōō vētshē'nō?

9

INFO The police in Italy are divided into three forces: the **carabinieri** käräbēnye're, the **polizia** pōlētsē'ä, and the **vigili urbani** vē'jēlē ōōrbä'nē. The **vigili urbani** are responsible for traffic and the stores in the towns. The **polizia** and the **carabinieri** have almost identical duties, but the **carabinieri** work under the auspices of the military, and the **polizia** answer to the civil authorities.

227

Does anyone here speak English?	**C'è qualcuno che parla inglese?** tshe kōō-älkōō'nō ke pär'lä ēn-gle'se?
I'd like to report ...	**Vorrei denunciare ...** vōre'ē denōōntshä're ...
a theft.	**un furto.** ōōn fōōr'tō.
an accident.	**un incidente.** ōōn ēntshēden'te.
a rape.	**uno stupro.** ōō'nō stōō'prō.
My *daughter/son* has disappeared.	*Mia figlia/Mio figlio* è ♀scomparsa/ ♂scomparso. mē'ä fē'lyä/mē'ō fē'lyō e ♀skōmpär'sä/♂skōmpär'sō.
My ... has been stolen.	**Mi hanno rubato ...** mē ä'nō rōōbä'tō ...
I've lost ...	**Ho perso ...** ō per'sō ...
My car has been broken into.	**Hanno forzato la mia macchina.** ä'nō fōrtsä'tō lä mē'ä mä'kēnä.
My *room/house* has been broken into.	**Qualcuno è etrato nella mia *casa/ camera.*** kōō-älkōō'nō e eträ'tō ne'lä mē'ä *kä'sä/kä'merä.*
I need a copy of the official report for insurance purposes.	**Mi occorre una copia della denuncia per la mia assicurazione.** mē ōkō're ōō'nä kō'pyä de'lä denōōn'tshä per lä mē'ä äsēkōōrätsyō'ne.
I'd like to speak to *my lawyer/the consulate.*	**Vorrei parlare con il mio *avvocato/ consolato.*** vōre'ē pärlä're kōn ēl mē'ō ävōkä'tō/kōnsōlä'tō.

228